TOWER HOUSE SCHOOL

Our World

THE EARTH IN SPACE

David Lambert

Wayland

Titles in this series

First published in 1988 by
Wayland (Publishers) Ltd
61 Western Road, Hove
East Sussex BN3 1JD, England

© Copyright 1988 Wayland (Publishers) Ltd

Edited by Kerstin Walker

Designed by Ross George

British Library Cataloguing in Publication Data
Lambert, David, 1932–
    The Earth in space. — (Our world).
    1. Planets — Juvenile literature
    I. Title   II. Series
    523.4   QB602

    ISBN 0-85078-945-1

Typeset by DP Press, Sevenoaks, Kent
Printed in Italy by G. Canale & C.S.p.A., Turin
Bound in Belgium by Casterman S.A.

Front cover, main picture The Earth in space.
Front cover, inset A photograph of Comet Bennett in 1970, which has had colour added.
Back cover Composite images of Saturn and her moons, taken from *Voyager*.

Contents

Discovering the Earth

Ancient Egyptians believed the Earth was a flat disc floating on a mighty sea. Egyptian and Babylonian priest-astronomers worshipped the Sun and Moon as gods, and thought the stars were people and animals in the sky. For, long ago, the universe seemed full of mystery.

Later, Greek astronomers and philosophers began to question such ideas. Some noticed how departing ships disappeared below the horizon. This surely hinted that the surface of the Earth was curved, not flat. More than 2,200 years ago Eratosthenes measured the curve. He compared the angle of the midday Sun in north and south Egypt and worked out that the Earth must be a giant ball with a circumference of 40,000 km – a figure now known to be almost correct.

But philosophers such as Plato and Aristotle believed the Earth stood at the centre of the universe. Circling the Earth, they said, were the Sun, the wandering planets and a great star-studded 'bowl' or sphere. Such notions lasted more than a thousand years.

Then European explorers and scientists began to gain a truer picture of the universe. By AD 1520 a ship had sailed the world and proved it to be round. In 1543 the Polish astronomer Nicolaus Copernicus revived an old idea that the Earth is not the centre of the universe, just one of several planets that revolve around the Sun. In the early 1600s Johannes Kepler, a German, showed that planets travel not in circles but in long, looping paths called ellipses.

Since then powerful telescopes and space probes have taught us much, much more. We now know that the Earth is one of the smaller, denser planets orbiting the Sun. The Sun is a star of only average size and brilliance. Sun, planets and their moons make up a solar system. Our own solar system lies in a great star cluster or galaxy – one of millions.

An Egyptian papyrus shows the Earth as a flat disc with the goddess Nut (Heaven) and the god Geb (Earth).

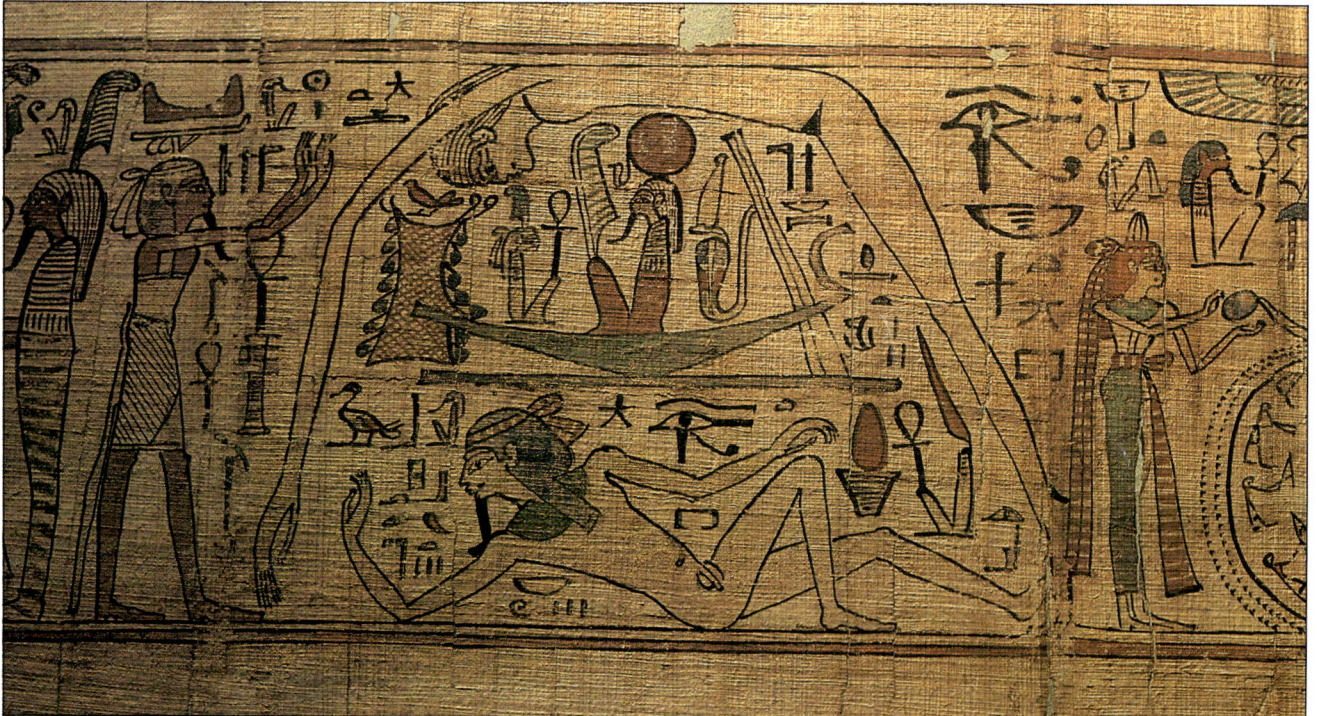

The Ptolemaic system of the universe showing the Earth in the centre, surrounded by air, water and fire.

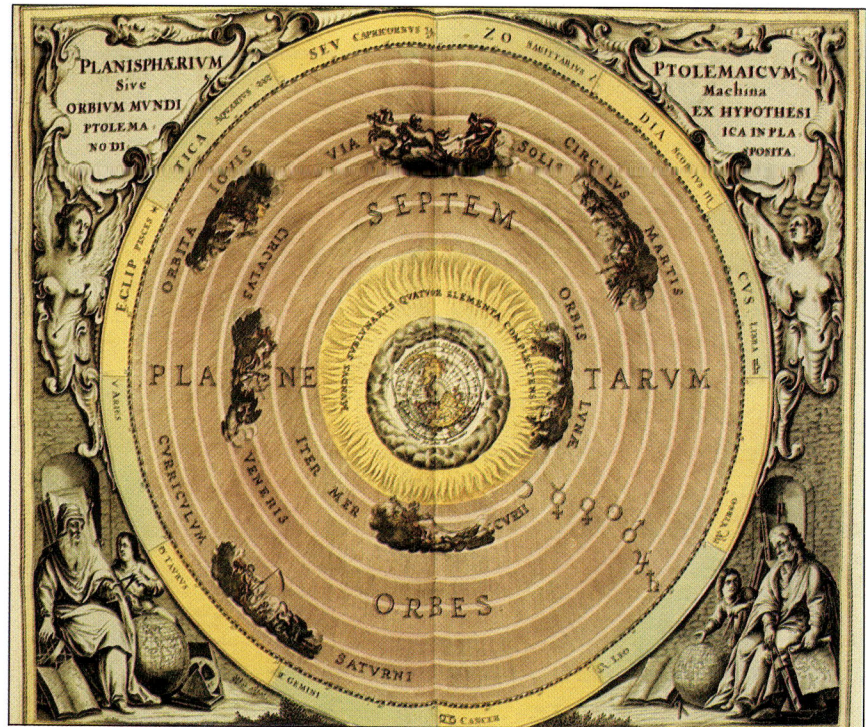

The Copernican system of the universe showing the Sun being circled by several planets, one of which is the Earth.

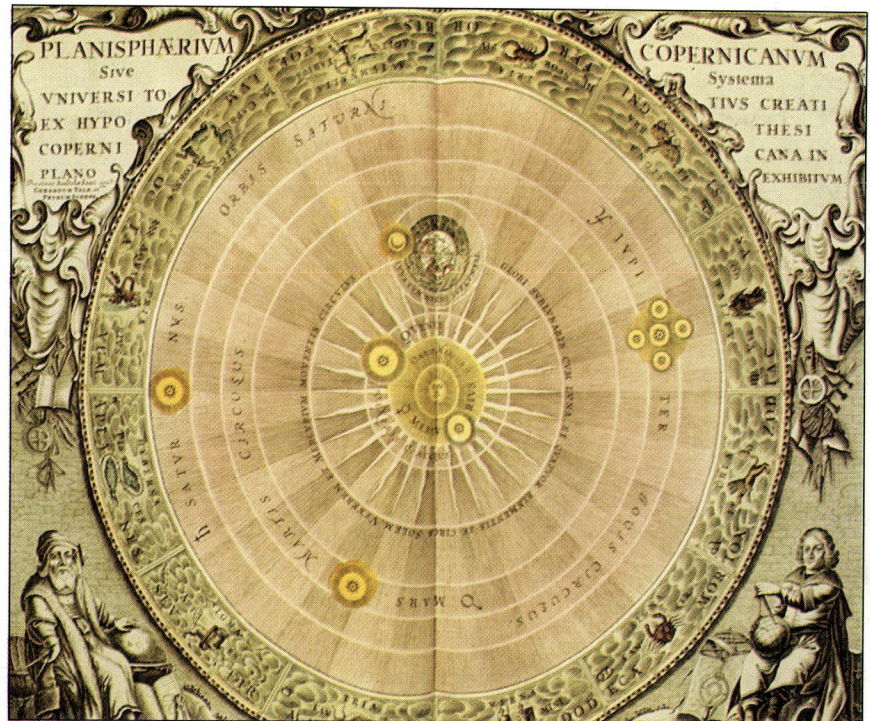

How the Earth began

Most scientists believe all stars and planets came into being with a vast explosion 20,000 million years ago. They think this Big Bang scattered matter at a tremendous speed through empty space. At first the only substances were tiny subatomic particles such as protons, neutrons and electrons. But only minutes after the Big Bang these began to come together, building hydrogen and helium atoms – the smallest, lightest, most abundant kinds of atoms known.

Millions of years later clouds of hydrogen gas shrank inwards under the force called gravitation. Shrinking heated up huge blobs of gas until it set off nuclear reactions. These turned hydrogen to helium and gave off heat and light. The blobs of gas began to shine as stars.

As stars used up their hydrogen they started 'burning' helium, and swelled up into so-called red giants. Some huge stars were destroyed in a vast explosion up to a hundred million times brighter than the Sun. One such star is called a supernova. Red giants and supernovae were the 'factories' where nuclear reactions fused the hearts of lighter atoms to build new, heavier kinds of atoms.

Now atoms of a single kind make up an element – a chemical substance that cannot be divided. About ninety elements make up the Earth and all that it contains. Carbon, nitrogen and oxygen, and almost all the other elements that we are made of, were originally formed inside the fiery furnaces of distant stars. (Only hydrogen and some helium are older than the stars.)

Scientists believe that the red giants and supernovae shed their new elements into space. About 5,000 million years ago trillions of atoms of these elements collected in a cold, flat, spinning disc of dust and gas inside our galaxy. The middle of this disc condensed and heated up to form our glowing, gas-rich Sun. Farther out, the disc shrank into blobs of dust and gas that formed the planets and their moons.

6

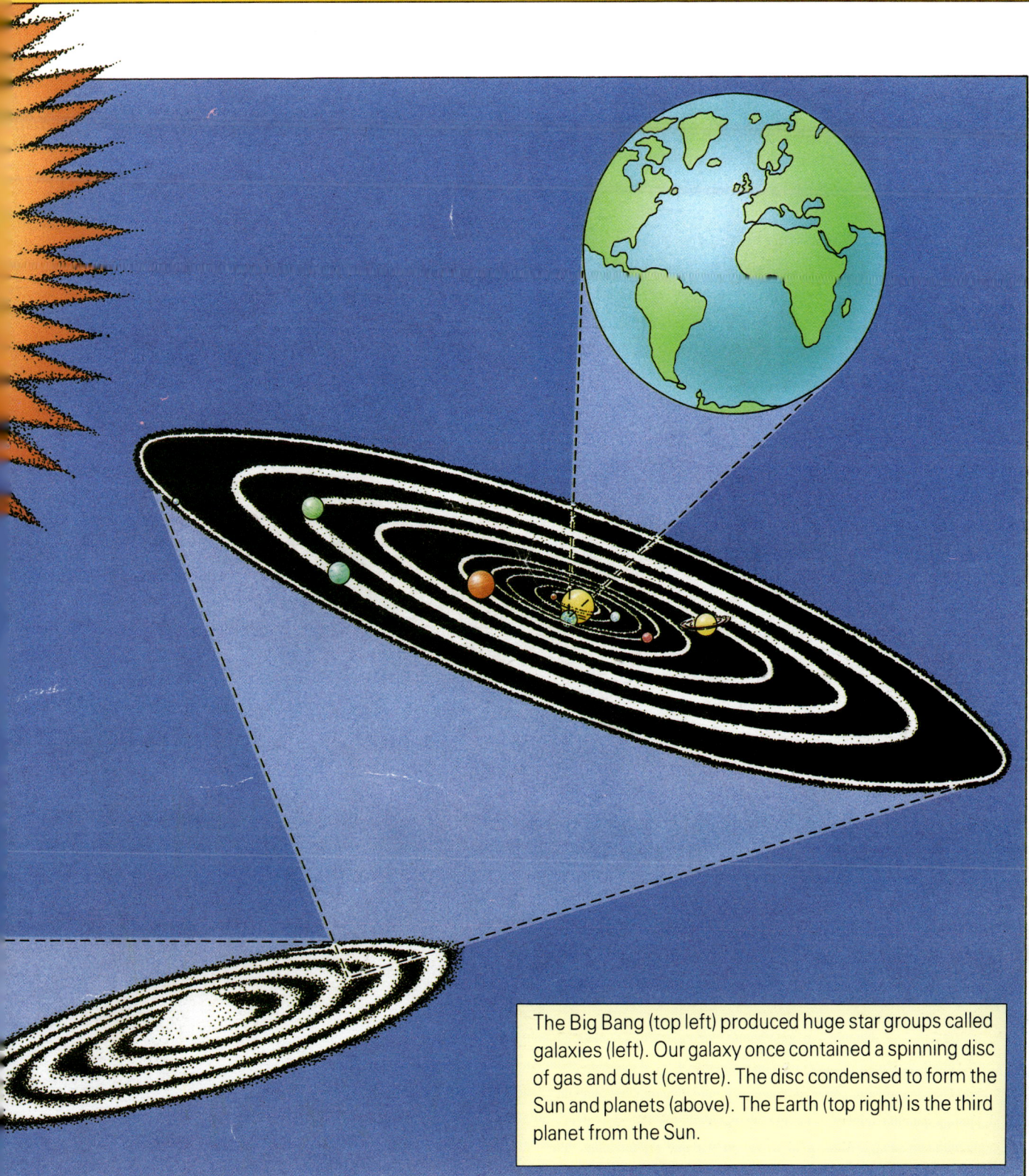

The Big Bang (top left) produced huge star groups called galaxies (left). Our galaxy once contained a spinning disc of gas and dust (centre). The disc condensed to form the Sun and planets (above). The Earth (top right) is the third planet from the Sun.

The layered Earth

Scientists now know that our world is made up of layers rather like an onion. They think the Earth formed from dust and gas.

First, dust grains came together as they whizzed around the Sun. Dust grains clumped together into rocky lumps. Small lumps stuck to large lumps that grew into mini planets known as planetesimals. Small planetesimals, about 100 km across, crashed into bigger ones and made these larger still. After a million years or so swarms of joining planetesimals formed the Earth, about 4,600 million years ago.

Meanwhile gravity was sorting out the Earth's materials. Dense elements like iron and nickel sank into the middle and became intensely hot as they were squashed by substances above. Lighter elements such as oxygen and silicon bobbed up to the surface. Above this a film of gases formed the early atmosphere.

Five main layers form the Earth today. The outer layer is air, an invisible atmosphere of mixed gases, mainly nitrogen and oxygen. Most of the atmosphere lies lower than the highest mountains.

A slice cut from the Earth shows the different thicknesses of crust, mantle, outer core and inner core.

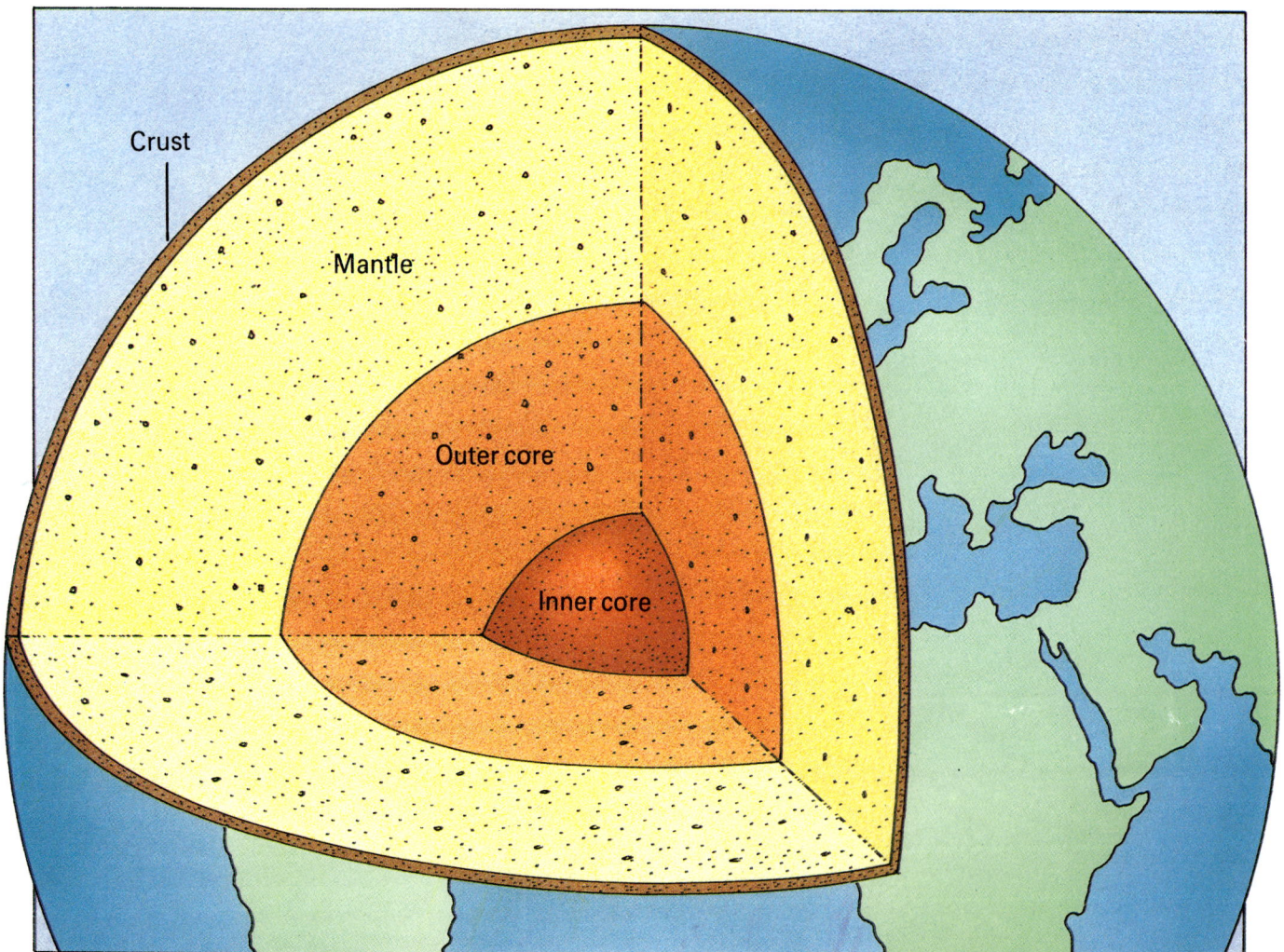

Crust

Mantle

Outer core

Inner core

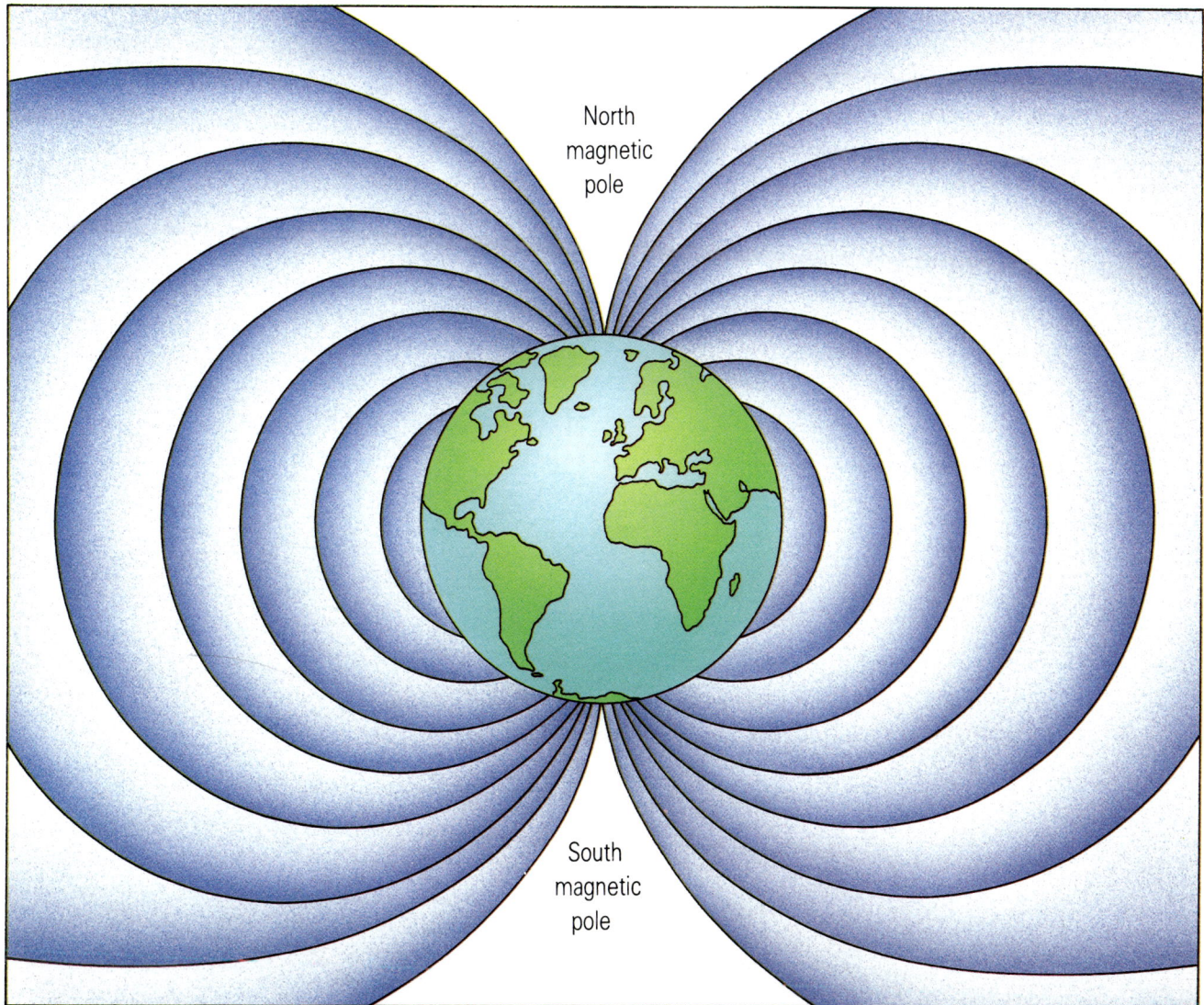

North
magnetic
pole

South
magnetic
pole

The Earth has a magnetic field with invisible lines of force. These form a pattern around our planet much like the pattern iron filings make around a bar magnet.

Next comes the solid crust of rocks rich in silicon and oxygen. This layer is only up to 50 km thick.

Below the light rocks of the crust lie the mantle's denser, hotter rocks. Earthquake vibrations passing through the Earth indicate that the mantle layer is about 2,900 km thick.

Below the mantle lies the Earth's molten outer core. This mainly iron and nickel layer is about 2,240 km thick. Streams of molten metal in the outer core create electric currents that make the Earth magnetic, with magnetic poles that keep compass needles pointing roughly north and south.

Below the outer core comes the inner core. This is probably a ball of solid iron and nickel 2,400 km across. The inner core is heated to perhaps 3,700 °C, but cannot melt because of pressure from above.

The Earth's changing surface

The surface of the Earth is never still. Air, oceans, continents and ocean floors are always on the move.

Scientists believe the Earth's crust is like an ever-shifting jigsaw made of pieces known as crustal plates. Some carry continents and some are slabs of ocean floor. The energy that shifts these plates around is heat escaping from the Earth's core and mantle.

Scientists also believe that currents of molten rock rise through the mantle, rather like boiling water in a saucepan. The currents hit the thin crust below ocean floors, and then divide. This pushes up and pulls apart the ocean crust to form great underwater mountain chains called spreading ridges. Rising molten rock fills cracks along each ridge then cools to form new ocean floor. This creeps slowly sideways from the ridge until it meets and dives below another crustal plate. Ocean floor is always being made and lost through these processes. No plate lasts longer than about 200 million years. Colliding plates fold up parts of continents into mountain ranges. Here, too, volcanoes grow and earthquakes shake the land.

Meanwhile, energy in the form of sunshine is beaming down upon the Earth's surface from above. Sunshine warms the atmosphere and the upper surface of the crust unevenly. In hot lands warm air rises and spreads out towards the cooler

A cutaway of part of the Earth to show plate movements. (1) Currents of molten rock (magma) rise through the mantle where two plates meet. (2) Magma cools and hardens to form new crustal rock along the ocean ridge. The plates are pulled apart. (3) In 'subduction zones' two plates push against each other. One is forced down under the other and melts to form magma. (4) Magma may rise through the overlying plate to form volcanoes on the surface. (5) Plates collide under mountain ranges forcing rocks to fold up.

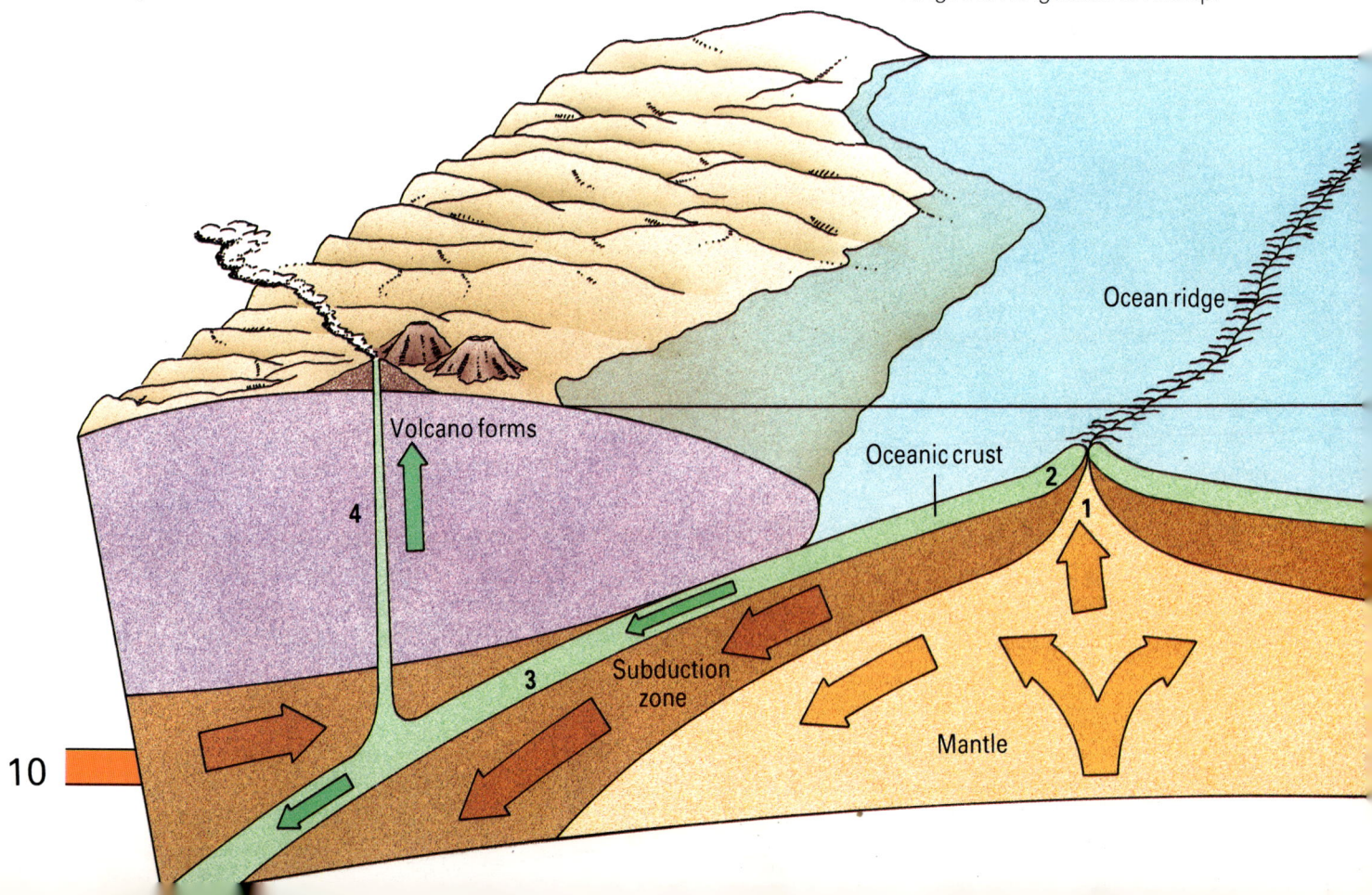

Volcano forms

Ocean ridge

Oceanic crust

Subduction zone

Mantle

regions. The cooling air grows heavier and sinks, then flows back to its starting place. This produces winds. Winds drive waves and currents through the oceans. Together moving air and water spread the Sun's heat more evenly around the Earth's surface.

The Sun's heat also evaporates moisture from land and sea, which will later fall as rain. Rain feeds rivers that wash away the surface of the land. When a river reaches the sea, mud and sand taken from the land are dumped in the estuary. In time this sediment forms layered rocks like shale and sandstone. Millions of years later, colliding crustal plates may thrust these rocks up to build new land.

Right Following a storm this waterfall in the Brecon Beacons, Wales, has been coloured red by the underlying bedrock of old red sandstone. The river will carry this sediment out to sea and dump it in the estuary.

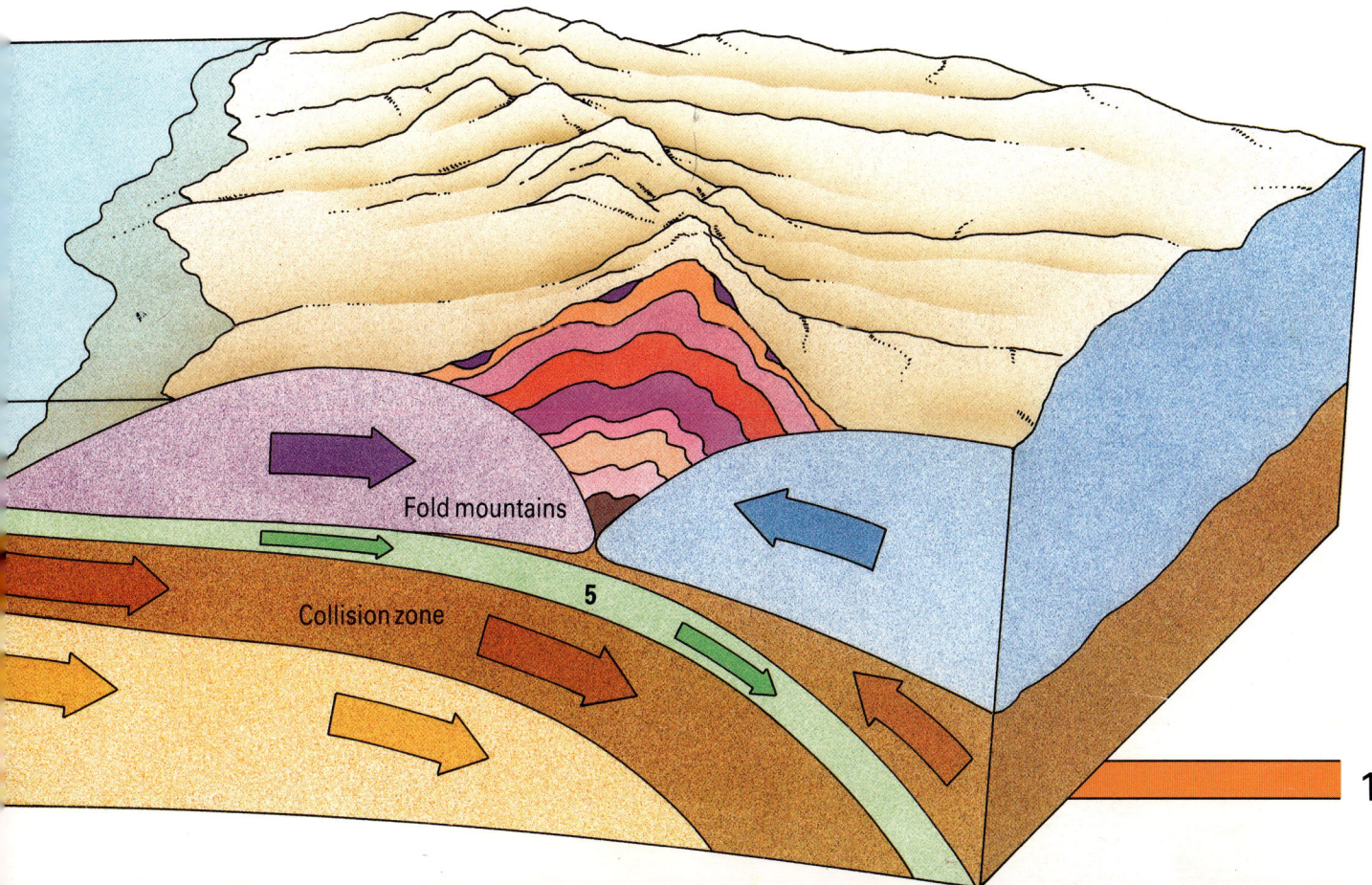

Fold mountains

Collision zone

5

How living things evolved

As far as we know the Earth is the only planet with living organisms. The other planets in our solar system seem unsuitable for life – being either too hot, too cold, too dry, or with gases that are unfit to breathe.

It has been estimated that as many as 980 million kinds of plants and animals have lived upon the Earth since it began. Maybe 4.5 million species are alive today. The rest have become extinct. But many left fossils in layered rocks – usually the lower the layer, the older the fossils. Fossils are the clues that show how living things evolved into the kinds we see around today.

The first living things were probably microscopic one-celled organisms like bacteria, drifting in the sea perhaps 4,000 million years ago. By 1,000 million years ago, the sea held tiny plants, producing food from chemicals and releasing oxygen as waste. This gas helped shut out harmful radiations from the Sun and made the atmosphere breathable for animals – many-celled organisms depending on plants for their food.

Fossil remains of *Archaeopteryx*, the flying reptile with feathers, or the earliest known bird, found in Bavaria. It is seen as the link between reptile and bird.

By 700 million years ago jellyfish, worms and other soft-bodied creatures swam or crawled about the seas. Some evolved into sea creatures protected by an outer shell or supported by an inner skeleton. Fish, the first backboned animals, appeared by 500 million years ago.

Later, plants and animals invaded the land. Here, fish with lungs evolved into amphibians that were related to today's frogs and salamanders. Amphibians must lay their eggs in water. But one group of amphibians gave rise to reptiles – cold-blooded, scaly creatures mostly hatched from eggs laid on land. Some reptiles evolved into the birds. About 190 million years ago other reptiles evolved into mammals, which are warm-blooded, hairy creatures. Humans are mammals.

From time to time, mysterious disasters wiped out thousands of species of animals and plants. But all the main groups of plants and animals survived.

Right This path of life names the aeons and periods when new forms of life appeared on Earth.

Left The European or fire salamander with its young.

ARCHAEAN AEON

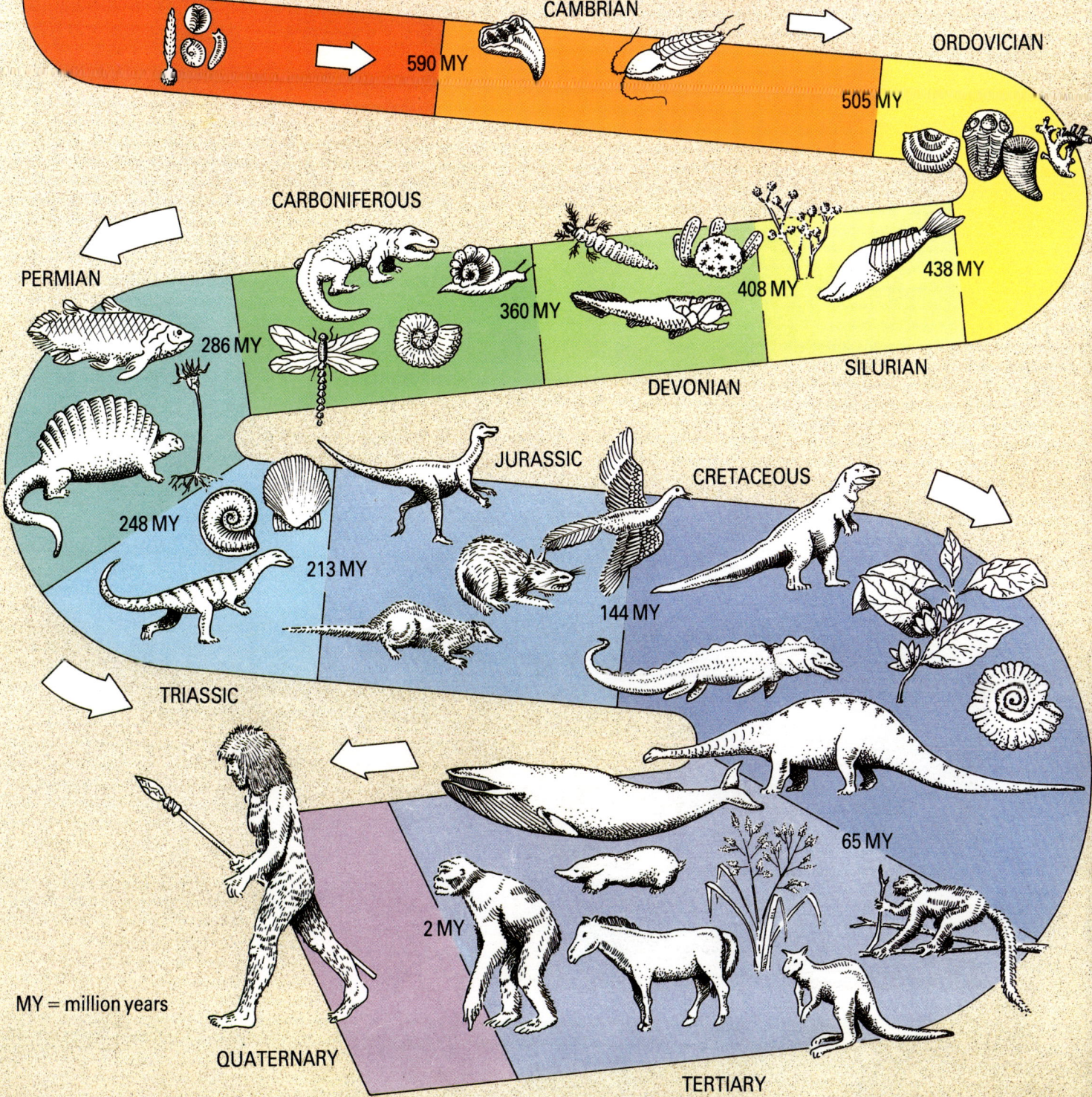

PROTEROZOIC AEON

CAMBRIAN

590 MY

ORDOVICIAN

505 MY

CARBONIFEROUS

PERMIAN

286 MY

360 MY

408 MY

438 MY

DEVONIAN

SILURIAN

JURASSIC

CRETACEOUS

248 MY

213 MY

144 MY

TRIASSIC

65 MY

2 MY

QUATERNARY

TERTIARY

MY = million years

Life today

Living things thrive only in the biosphere – a thin film of water, air and land clinging to the outer edge of our planet.

The highest flying birds soar no higher than the thin, cold, mountain air. The highest plants are windswept mountain mosses and lichens. Most land plants and animals live in the warmer, denser air of valleys, plains and lower mountain slopes.

Most ocean life is concentrated near the sunlit surface. Here tiny plants form food for billions of tiny animals that in turn are hunted by whales and fish. No plants survive the deep, dark ocean depths. But deep-sea fish feed upon dead creatures that have sunk to the sea-bed.

The world holds several hundred thousand kinds of plants and maybe several million kinds of animals, mostly insects. Each kind is suited to particular conditions. Palm trees and monkeys flourish in rainy tropical forests, while dwarf willows and polar bears endure the cold Arctic region. Each natural region, including mountains,

The polar bear has a thick coat of fur to protect it against the Arctic cold.

Below Zebra and springbuck on the dry plains of the savanna in Namibia, Africa.

deserts, savannas, temperate grasslands and temperate and cold forests, has its special plants and animals.

Certain groups of animals live only in one continent or area, separated from the rest by sea, mountains or deserts. Zoologists divide the world into a number of such areas, called realms.

Unlike most creatures humans now inhabit every region of the world. A complex brain and nimble fingers help us to survive almost anywhere. Our inventions have helped us to change the surface of the Earth to suit our needs. Saws and ploughs are used to turn forests into food-producing farmlands. Drills burrow into rocks for fuels or minerals such as coal, oil, iron and copper. In factories these are converted into useful products such as cans, cars and refrigerators.

But overuse is damaging the world – destroying wild plants and animals, creating deserts, and polluting air and shallow seas. Unless we take more care we might well wreck our fragile home, the biosphere.

The natural habitat of the brown howler monkey is in the dense vegetation of the tropical rainforest.

Below The Bingham copper mine in the USA is an example of human activity changing the natural world.

Earth and Sun

Earth is the planet third nearest the Sun, 150 million kilometres away. Four of the nine planets in our solar system are larger than our own, but none is denser – our planet's density is 5.5 times that of water. Our planet is less than a millionth the size of the Sun, whose vast mass acts like a magnet that stops our speeding world from escaping into space. Instead, we travel around the Sun, which gives us day and night, the year, and seasons.

Seen from space the Earth roughly resembles a giant ball, with a circumference of 40,000 km. This ball spins about an axis. We call the ends of the axis the North and South Poles. Its spin makes the Earth bulge slightly near the equator – an imaginary line around its middle.

At this point in the Earth's orbit it is night-time in most of North America and day in South America.

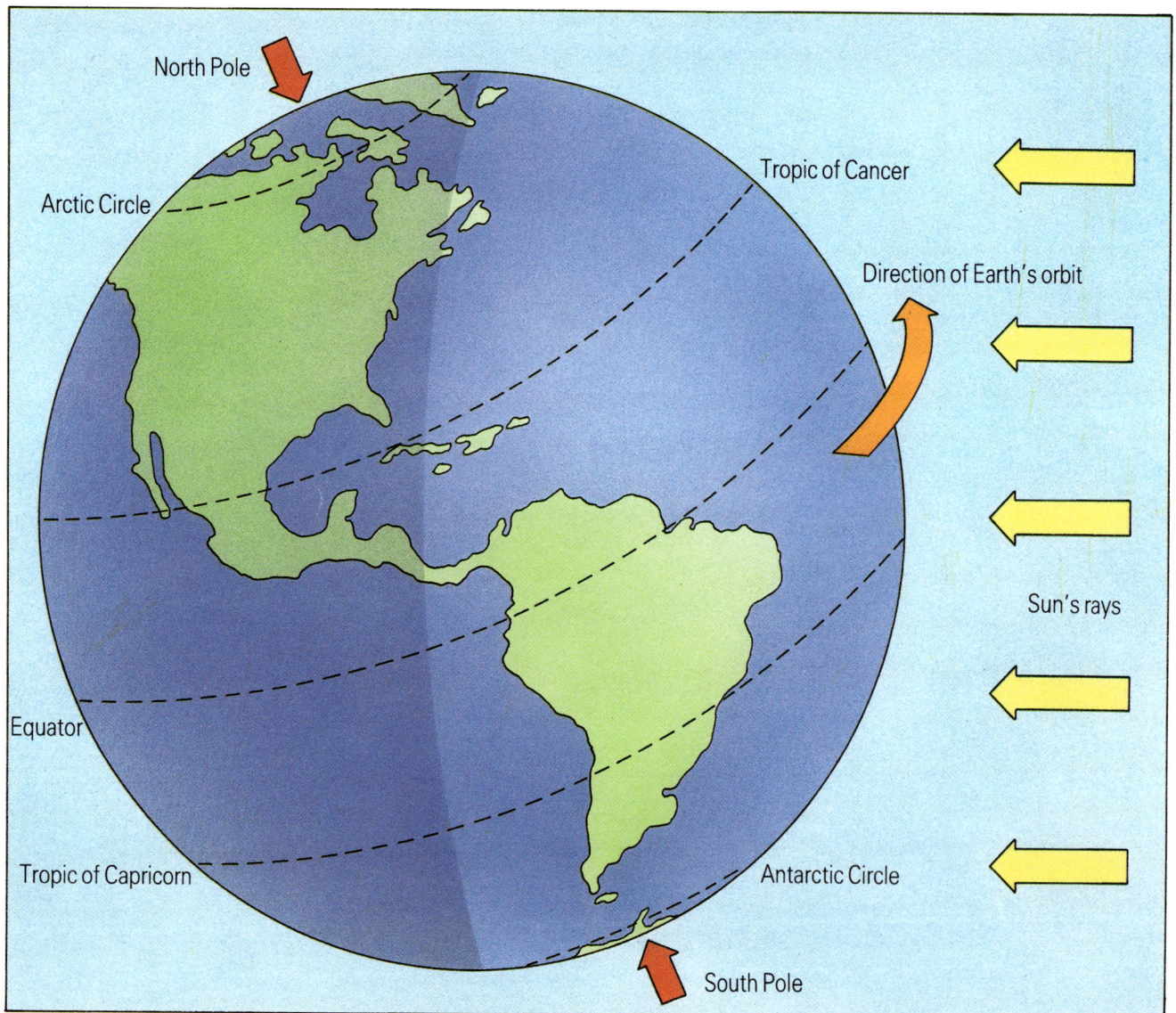

North Pole

Arctic Circle

Tropic of Cancer

Direction of Earth's orbit

Sun's rays

Equator

Tropic of Capricorn

Antarctic Circle

South Pole

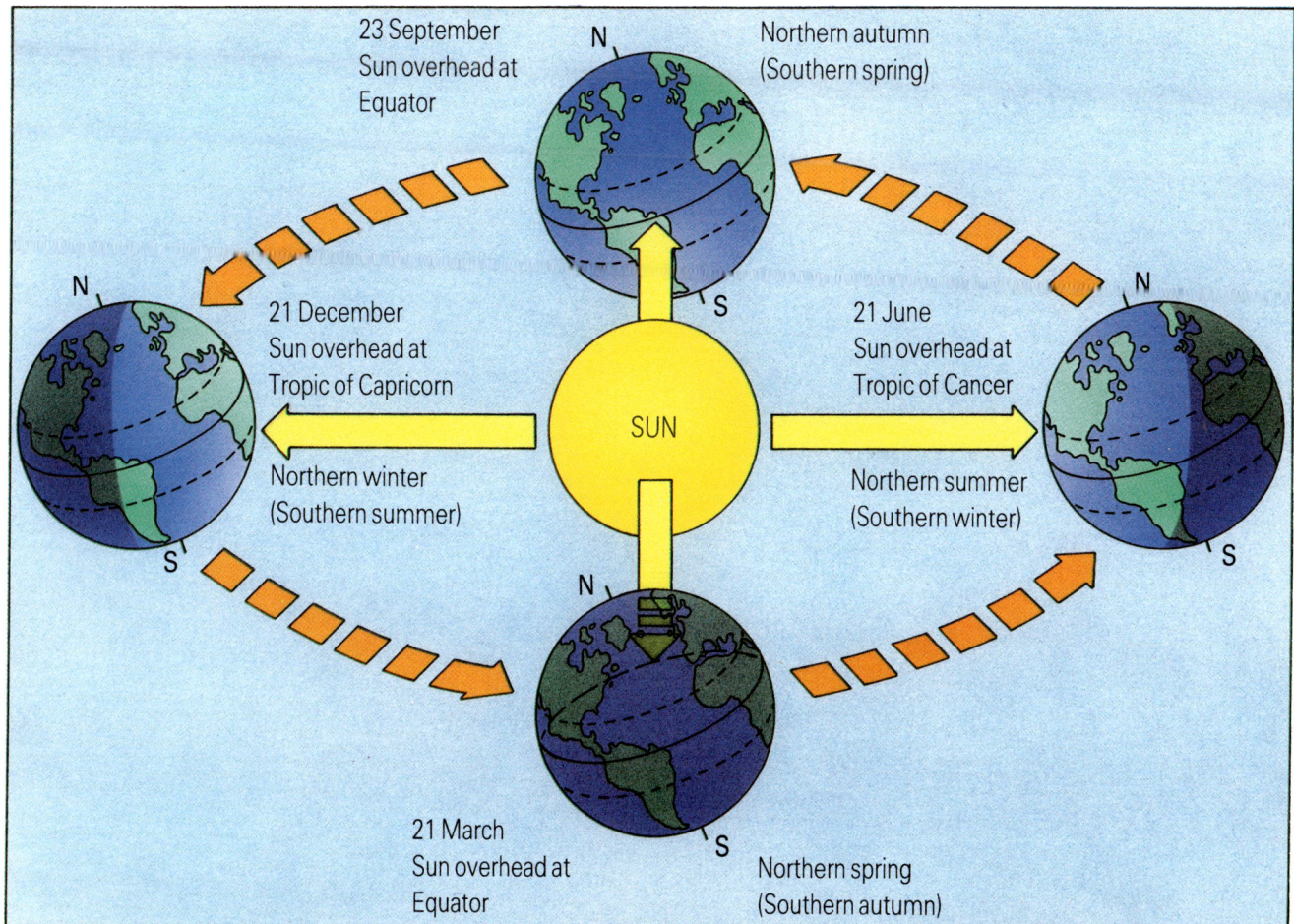

23 September
Sun overhead at
Equator

Northern autumn
(Southern spring)

N

S

21 December
Sun overhead at
Tropic of Capricorn

N

Northern winter
(Southern summer)

S

SUN

21 June
Sun overhead at
Tropic of Cancer

N

Northern summer
(Southern winter)

S

N

S

21 March
Sun overhead at
Equator

Northern spring
(Southern autumn)

The Earth at different seasons in one annual orbit of the Sun. The Earth's tilt brings the Sun overhead at different places in the tropics at different times of year.

Our planet completes one turn about every 24 hours – a day and night. It is day on the Earth's Sun-facing side, night on the side in shadow. Because the world spins eastward, the Sun seems to rise in the east and sink in the west.

Our planet zooms around the Sun at 29.8 km/sec, completing each orbit in about 365 days – one Earth year. Because the Earth is tilted, the North and South Poles lean towards the Sun at different times of the year. On about 21 March the Sun's rays shine straight down on the equator. On this day the length of day and night are equal everywhere and spring starts in the northern hemisphere. On about 21 June the Sun is directly above the Tropic of Cancer, an imaginary line about a quarter of the way from the equator to the North Pole. On this day the northern hemisphere has its longest day and starts its summer. On about 21 September the Sun is back above the equator, and the northern autumn starts. On about 21 December the Sun is overhead at the Tropic of Capricorn, about one quarter the way from the equator to the South Pole. The north has its shortest day and starts its winter. In the southern hemisphere seasons are reversed.

The Sun

Compared to many stars the Sun is small. Yet this glowing ball is much the biggest, hottest and brightest object in our solar system.

Astronomers say the Sun has a diameter of nearly 1,400,000 km – more than 100 times that of the Earth. It fills more space than 1,300,000 Earth-sized planets. If you could weigh them both, the Sun would be more than 330,000 times heavier than the Earth. Also its pulling force, or gravitation, is nearly 30 times that of the Earth.

Yet, bulk for bulk, the Sun is light. Its density is about one quarter that of the Earth. This is because, like most stars, the Sun is composed mainly of hydrogen gas, the lightest substance known.

In the Sun's core, the nuclei, or centres of hydrogen atoms, are squashed until they fuse together like nuclei in a hydrogen bomb. A bomb takes seconds to explode, but the Sun's nuclear reaction has lasted nearly 5,000 million years. It could last as long again, even though the Sun loses four million tonnes in weight each second. Nuclear fusion gobbles up huge quantities of matter as it

A cutaway view of the Sun revealing the inner and outer regions. Nuclear reactions in its core make hot gas circulate like boiling water, squirting molten matter from the surface and beaming energy through space.

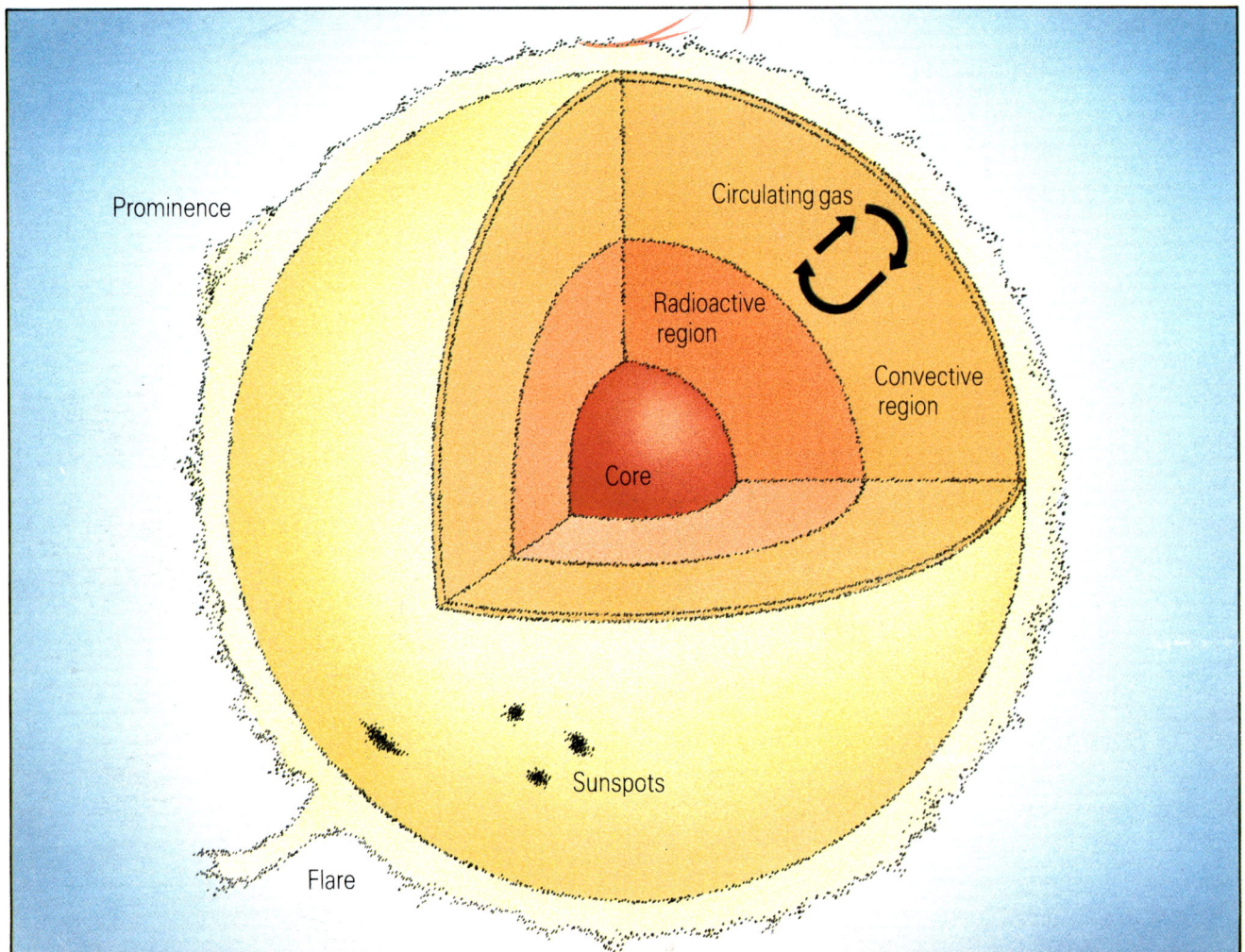

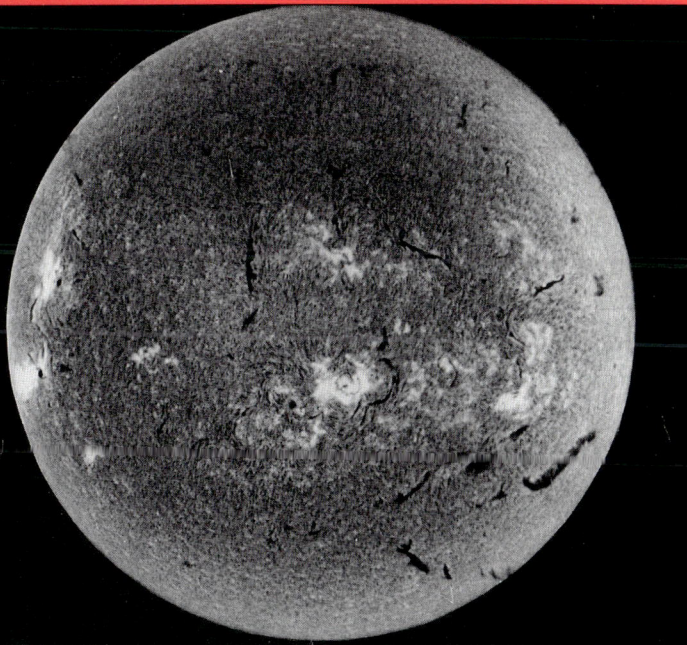

In this picture of the Sun the white areas are active regions and the black dots are sunspots. The filaments that appear as black lines are prominences when viewed at the edge of the Sun.

turns hydrogen into helium. Meanwhile the reaction releases vast quantities of heat, light and other energy; the Sun's core is 14,000°C.

Even the Sun's surface, the photosphere, is hot enough to melt iron. No wonder stars like ours beam light and heat far out across the universe. (The light from moons and planets is just reflected sunlight.) Dark sunspots in the photosphere are cooler patches caused by changes in the Sun's magnetic field. Sunspots may set tongues of blazing gas called solar flares leaping high into the chromosphere – the lower region of the solar atmosphere. The flares send a solar wind of electrically-charged particles streaming out through space. Bursts of glowing gas, called solar prominences, erupt thousands of kilometres into the solar corona, the Sun's outer atmosphere.

A picture of the Sun showing a burst of glowing gas erupting into the Sun's outer atmosphere.

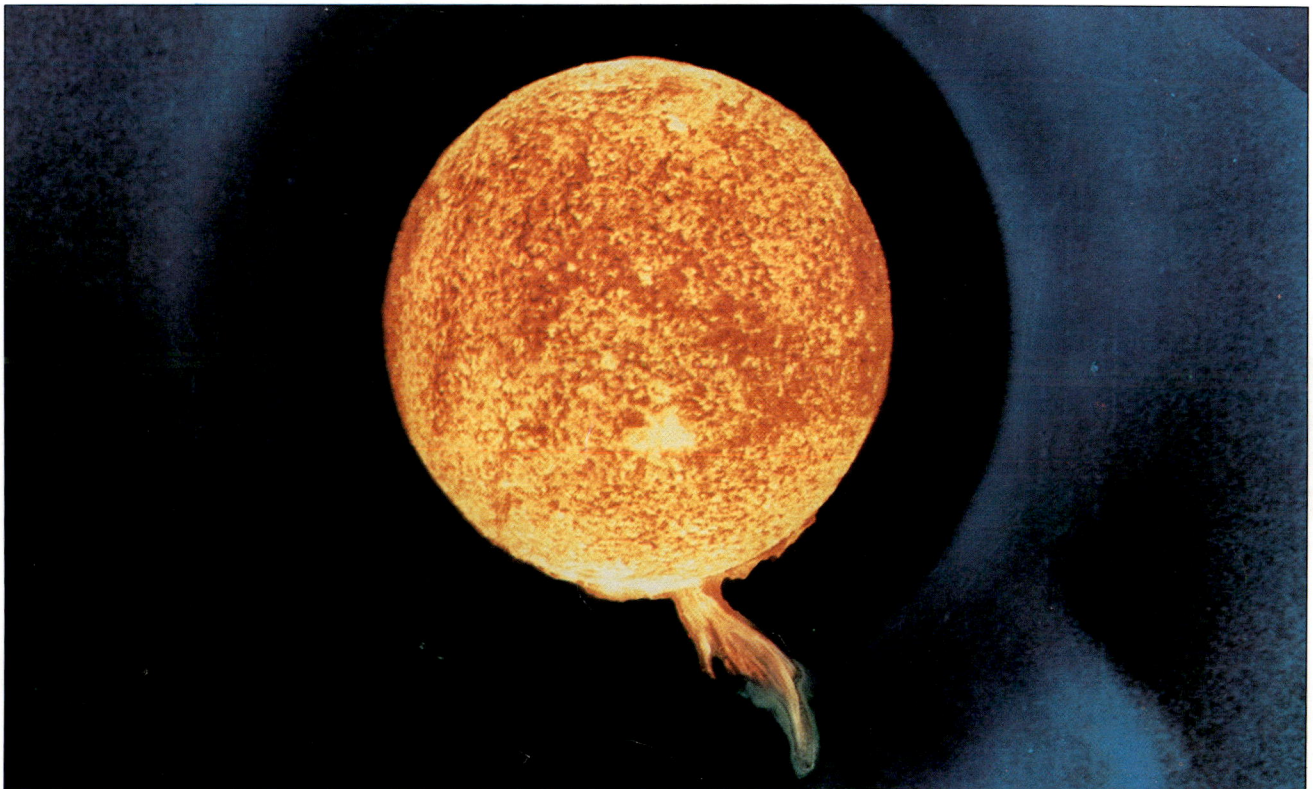

Earth and Moon

The Moon is the nearest neighbour to the Earth and is its only natural satellite. This ball of rock is much smaller than the Earth and tours around it, held there by the Earth's gravity. Only 376,000 km or so separate the two. The Moon is near enough to affect our world in several ways.

Tides happen because the Moon's gravitational pull lifts ocean waters into a bulge on the Earth's Moon-facing side. Another bulge occurs on the Earth's far side as the Moon pulls the Earth away from its water. As the Earth spins, both bulges travel around the oceans as high tides, with low tides between.

Reflected sunlight from the Moon gives us moonlight. But the actual amount of Moon we see varies with the changing angle that the orbiting Moon makes with the Earth and Sun. At the new Moon phase the Moon's Earth-facing side is dark. Next the Moon waxes (seems to grow) into a half Moon, then a full Moon. Then it wanes into a half Moon and returns to the new Moon phase. These changes take about a month. (The Moon revolves

Changing positions of the orbiting Moon produce the Moon's phases pictured at the bottom of the page. These are:
1 new moon, 2 crescent, 3 first quarter, 4 gibbous, 5 full, 6 gibbous, 7 last quarter, 8 crescent.

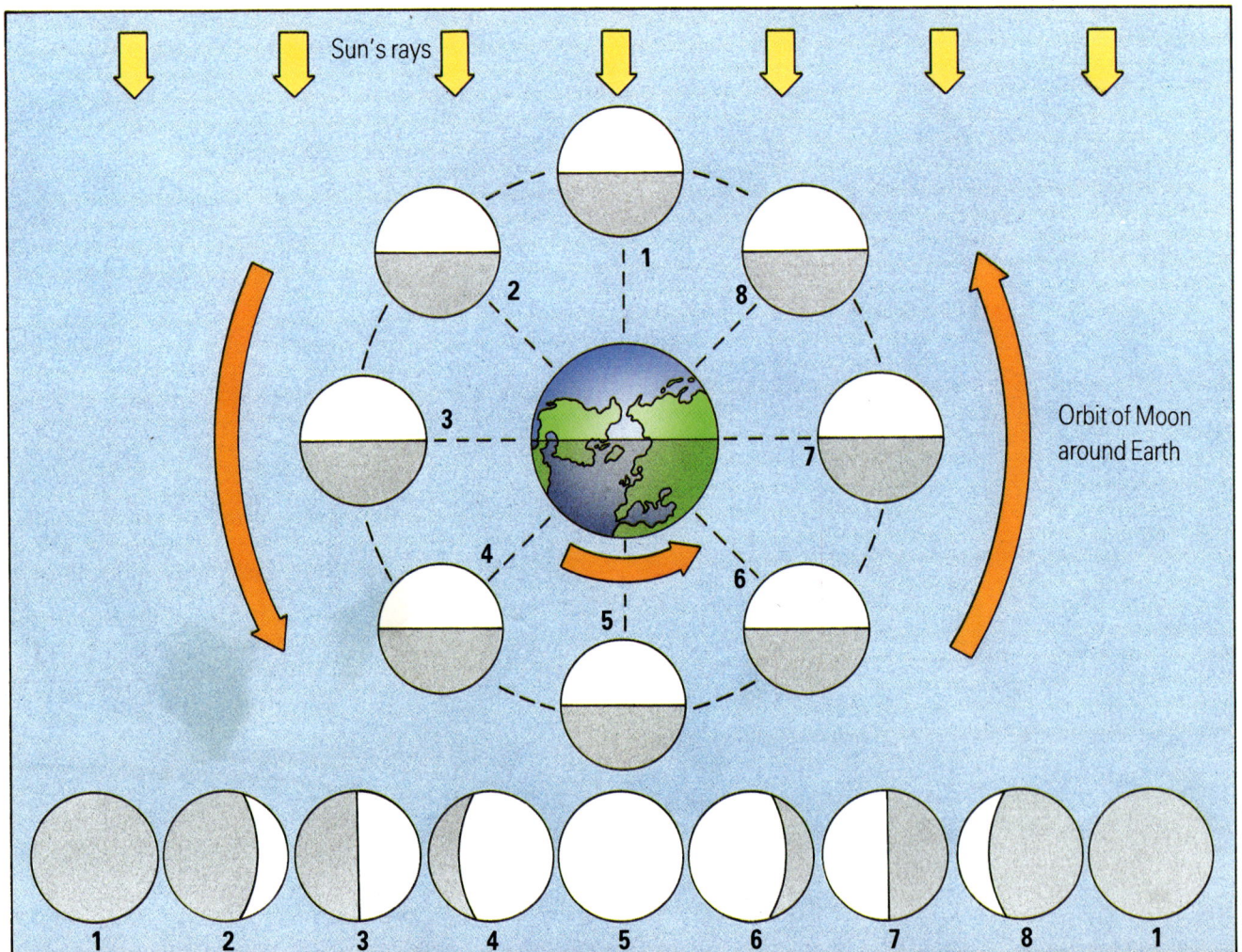

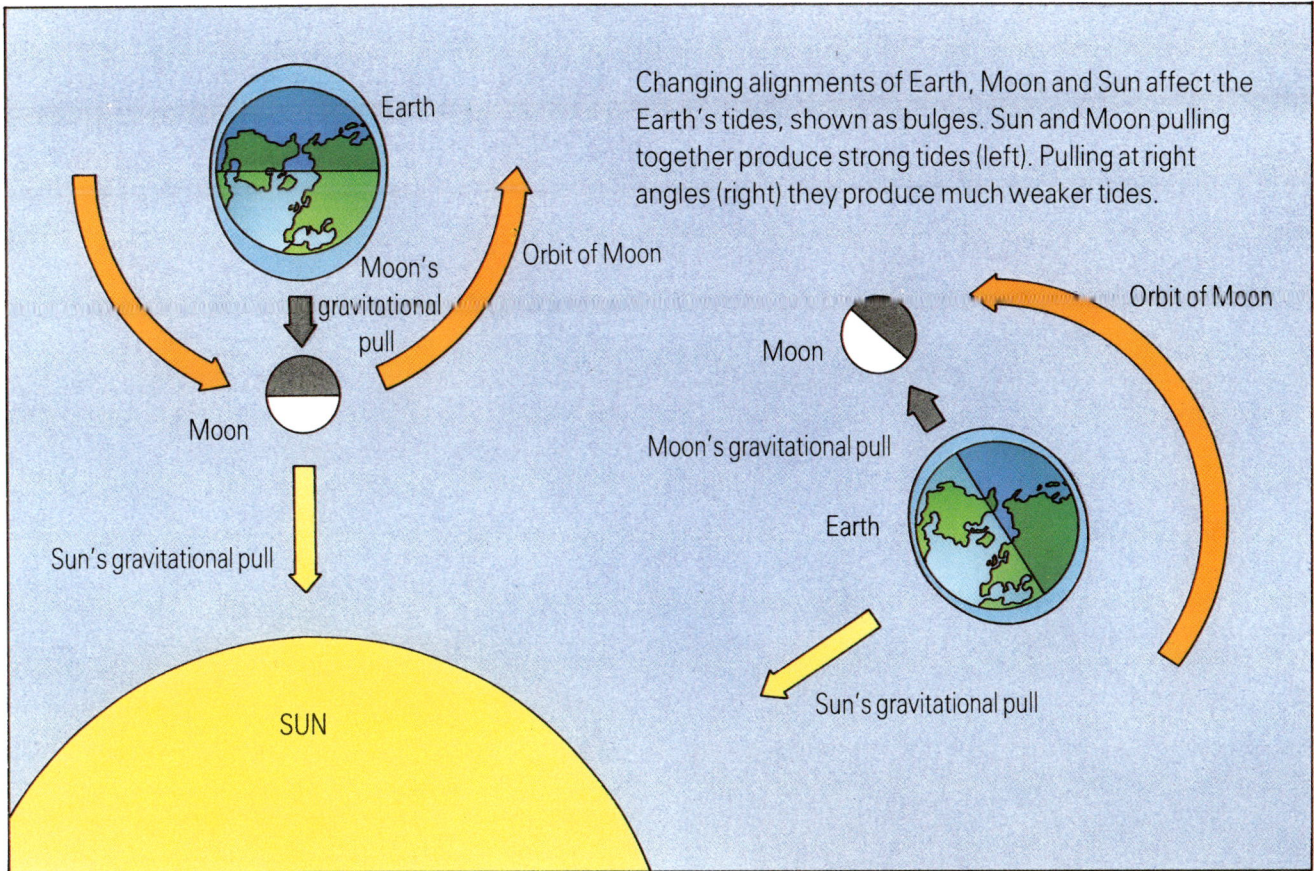

Changing alignments of Earth, Moon and Sun affect the Earth's tides, shown as bulges. Sun and Moon pulling together produce strong tides (left). Pulling at right angles (right) they produce much weaker tides.

only once in each orbit, so the same side always faces the Earth.)

Sometimes the Moon is positioned between the Sun and Earth and causes an eclipse. In a total solar eclipse the Moon completely hides the Sun from part of the Earth. Here the Moon's shadow makes the sky almost as dark as at night. In a partial solar eclipse, the Moon only partly hides the Sun, and the sky does not become so black. The Moon's shadow sweeps across the Earth so fast that solar eclipses last only a few minutes.

Lunar eclipses occur when the Earth is positioned between the Sun and Moon. Then the Earth's shadow darkens the Moon, sometimes for more than an hour and a half because the shadow that falls is so large.

In a solar eclipse the Moon comes between the Sun and Earth, and totally hides the Sun from part of the Earth.

The Moon

Thanks to telescopes and spacecraft we now know much about the Moon. We know its diameter is less than the distance across Australia. We know it occupies about one-fiftieth as much space as the Earth, and if you could weigh them both the Earth would be about 80 times heavier. A person on the Moon seems to weigh one-sixth as much as on the Earth, so low is the Moon's force of gravitation.

Without a spacesuit and other aids anyone would quickly die on the Moon for it lacks both air and water. Also it has hotter days and colder nights than any ever known on Earth.

Yet the lifeless Moon has altered greatly since it formed about the same time as the Earth. Dark areas, misleadingly called seas, are bone-dry plains of lava that welled up from the inside of the Moon several thousand million years ago. (Puzzlingly,

A picture of the full Moon taken from *Apollo 11*. The large dark areas are the 'seas', or dry plains of lava.

space probes show no such 'seas' on the Moon's far side.) Bright areas are mountain ranges made of rocks older even than the lava plains.

Craters with raised rims pock the surface everywhere. Some are small, but others are immense and very deep. The Orientale Basin measures about 960 km across, and the Newton Crater could be 8,000 m from floor to rim. Erupting volcanoes produced some craters, but most were punched into the Moon by lumps of rock that fell like bombs from space. These meteorites and asteroids struck the Moon hard enough to send blobs of molten rock splashing far beyond the crater rims. Old splashes show up as white rays of glassy rocks projecting from craters, such as can be seen on the Copernicus Crater.

Many moonquakes shake the surface of the Moon each year. Deep down there must be hot rock that moves around. Perhaps the Moon contains a mantle and a core like those inside the Earth.

Above The Moon is smaller than the Earth and has no atmosphere, no oceans and no living things.

Right US astronaut Edwin Aldrin descending from the lunar module, *Apollo 11*. It was the first manned lunar landing mission and was launched in July, 1969.

Right inset The far side of the Moon. The large central crater has a diameter of 80 km.

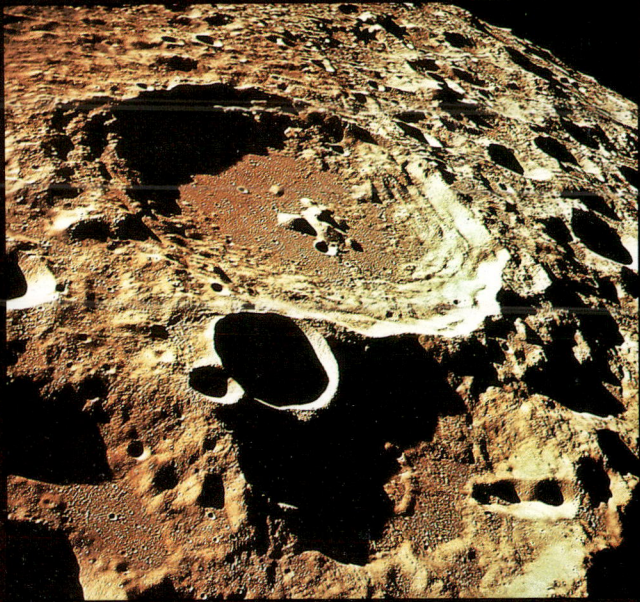

Mercury and Venus

Planets take their name from the Greek word for 'wanderers', because Ancient Greek astronomers noticed that these 'stars' moved against the background of the rest. In fact the planets are not stars, but shine by reflected sunlight.

All planets zoom anti-clockwise around the Sun, spaced out from it at different distances. Most lie on roughly the same plane. Some are orbited by moons. Each planet's length of day depends upon its rate of spin. Its year depends upon the time it takes to make one orbit of the Sun.

From the Sun outward the nine known planets are Mercury, Venus, Earth, Mars, Jupiter, Saturn, Uranus, Neptune and Pluto.

Mercury and Venus are small, dense planets with a solid crust. Neither has a moon. Mercury is the second smallest planet, about one-sixteenth the size of ours. Rugged mountains, craters and smooth lava plains make up its bare, rocky surface. There is scarcely any atmosphere. By day, Mercury gets hot enough for lead to melt. By night the surface is cold enough to turn oxygen into a liquid. Day and night last 59 times as long as ours, but a year is only 88 days long.

Venus lurks under thick, hot clouds made poisonous by sulphur. The bright sunshine reflected by these clouds earns Venus its other names of Evening Star and Morning Star. Below the orange sky lies a suffocating atmosphere of carbon dioxide gas. This gas traps the heat from sunshine,

The surface of Mercury, as shown by *Mariner 10*, is covered with craters. Because Mercury has no atmosphere asteroids pulled down from space did not break up. They plunged down and dug out craters.

and makes the rocky surface hotter than a kitchen cooker's hottest setting. Venus is mostly a flat, bare plain. The three highland areas include immense volcanoes and some are still active. This planet is almost as large as ours, but spins from east to west. Day and night on Venus are a little longer than its year, which lasts about 244 Earth days. This is because it takes longer to spin around its axis than it takes to go round the Sun.

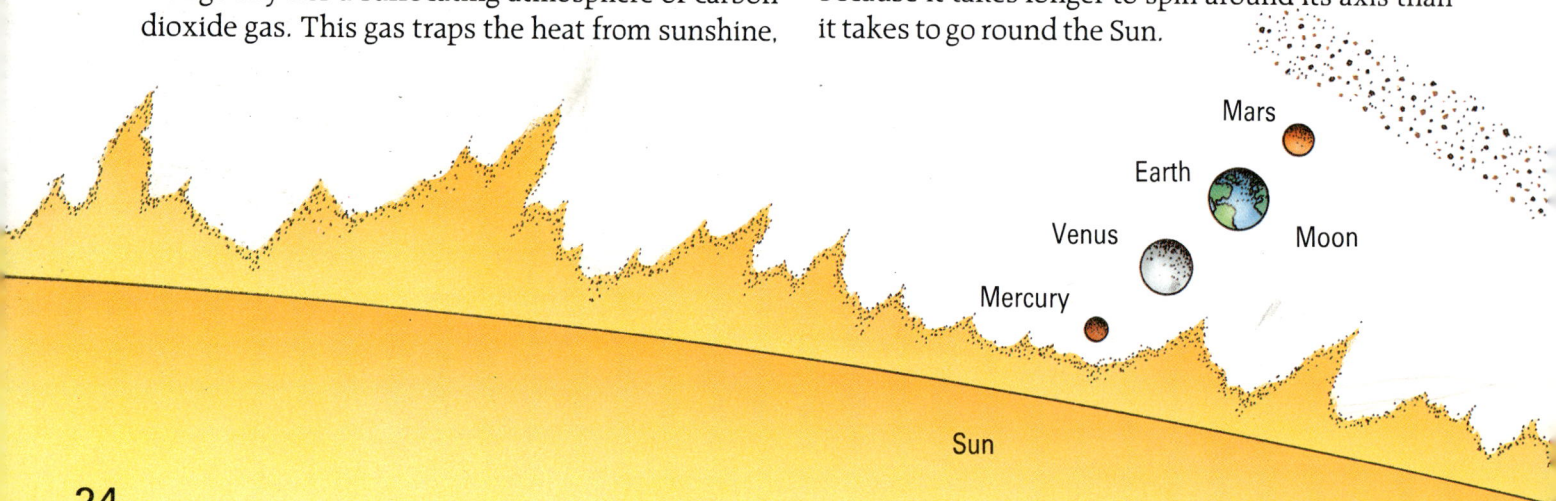

Mars

Earth

Venus

Moon

Mercury

Sun

The nine planets here appear to scale, but the distances between them are immense. Between Mars and Jupiter whizz lumps of rock called asteroids. Far beyond Pluto may lie a tenth planet. Astronomers think this could be five times heavier than the Earth, and orbiting at a different angle from all other planets.

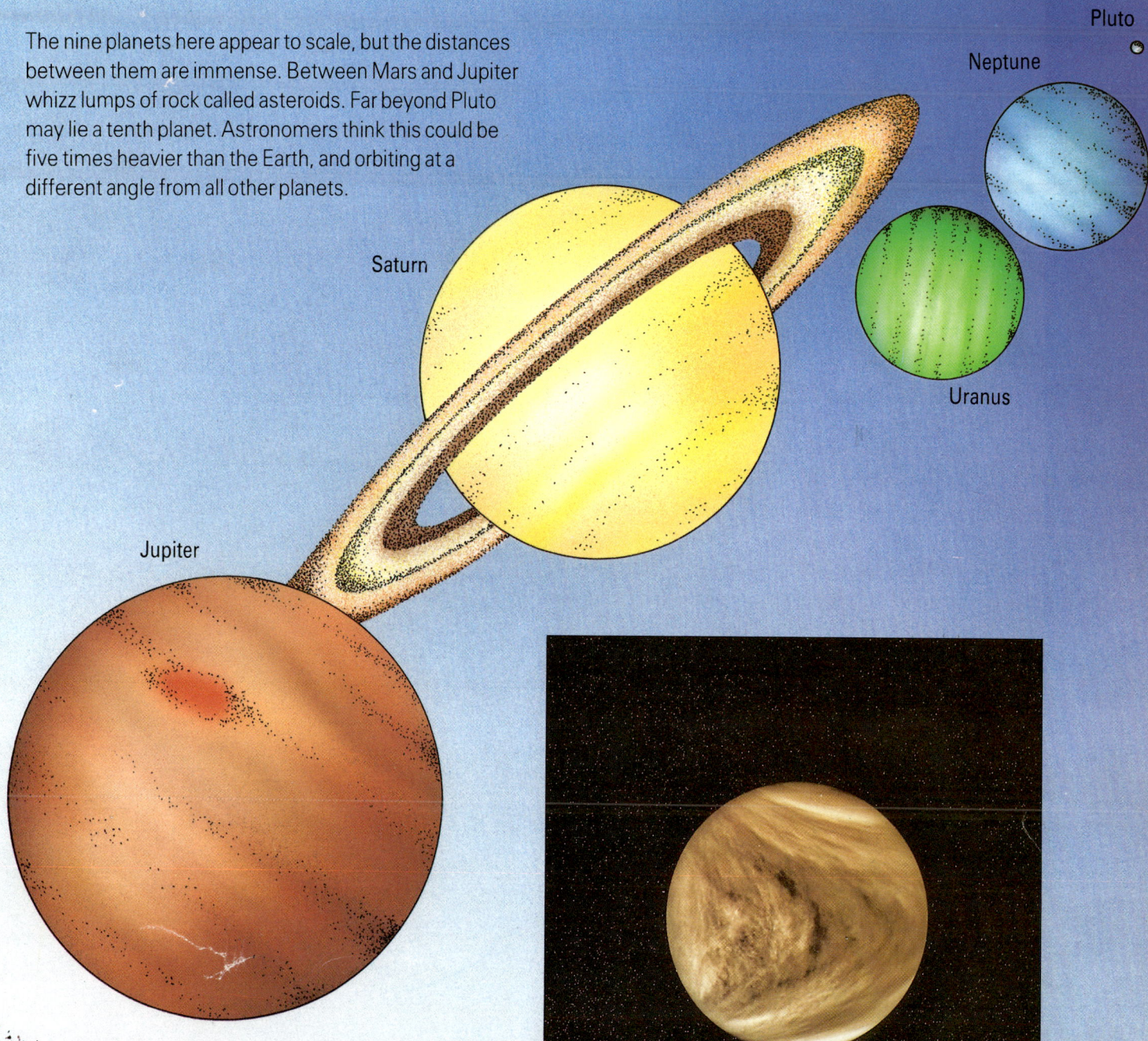

Pluto

Neptune

Saturn

Uranus

Jupiter

Asteroid belt

Right The surface of Venus is covered with a brilliant yellowish-white cloud. The surface temperature is 470°C, hotter than on any other planet.

25

Mars

The Romans named this blood-red planet after Mars, the Roman god of war. Mars is our nearest planetary neighbour after Venus. It is the first of the outer planets – the planets farther than the Earth is from the Sun.

Only two planets are smaller than Mars. Its volume – the space it occupies – is about one-seventh that of the Earth. The Earth's mass – the amount of matter it contains – is nine times that of Mars. This makes Martian gravitation low: a person on Mars would weigh little more than one-third as much as on Earth.

In some ways, Mars is the most Earth-like of the planets. Its day and night last about as long as ours. Mars orbits tilted like the Earth. This produces seasons. There are even polar ice caps that grow in winter and shrink in summer. But a Martian year lasts twice as long as ours.

Space probes show the surface to be dry and rugged. Much is reddish dust and rock, rather like the Arizona Desert in the USA. There are vast plains and plateaux. Craters cover half of Mars. Immense volcanoes rise from a vast swelling called the Tharsis Ridge. The giant volcano, Olympus Mons, is three times higher than Mount Everest. In places great cracks split the land. The Valles Marineris chasms form a gash far longer, deeper and wider than the Grand Canyon in the USA. There are also narrow twisting valleys carved by rivers long ago.

Once, Mars was warm, with liquid water, and perhaps enough air for living things to breathe. Now the Martian surface is bone dry, and gripped by Ice Age cold. All water lies frozen in ice caps or below ground. The atmosphere is thin and suffocating. Life on Mars seems impossible today.

Orbiting Mars are two small, lumpy moons called Phobos ('fear') and Deimos ('fright').

Right A photograph of a crescent Mars showing a plume of ice blowing from the volcano Ascreaus Mons.

Right Sunrise over the Noctis Labyrinthus, a region of canyons at the western end of the Valles Marineris, taken by *Viking Orbiter*.

Below This photograph of the Martian landscape, taken by *Viking Lander 2*, shows a surface covered by reddish dust, rocks and boulders.

Jupiter and Saturn

Jupiter and Saturn are giants among the nine planets. Jupiter is twice as large as all the rest would be if lumped together. Its volume is more than 1,300 times that of the Earth. Yet if you could weigh them both, Jupiter would be only 318 times heavier. This lightweight giant is not much denser than water. Scientists believe that Jupiter is mostly compressed hydrogen and helium gas. It has no solid surface.

Poisonous gases – methane and hydrogen sulphide – largely form the cloudy atmosphere. High up are bright white belts of ammonia gas. Between lie deeper, darker clouds tinged brown and orange by hydrogen sulphide ('bad egg gas').

Jupiter spins far faster than the Earth, and strong winds whirl its coloured belts of clouds around. Eddies in the atmosphere produce huge spiral 'storms'. One, the Great Red Spot, is even larger than the Earth.

Jupiter's day lasts less than half as long as ours, but its year is the equivalent of nearly twelve Earth years. More than a dozen moons orbit Jupiter. Four – Io, Europa, Ganymede and Callisto – are bigger than the smallest planet in the solar system, Pluto.

The mysterious planet Saturn is a flimsy giant more than half as large as Jupiter. Most of it consists of liquid hydrogen and helium, light enough to float on water. Fierce winds speed bands

Jupiter and two of its moons: the innermost satellite, Io, is set against the planet, and Europa is on the far right.

of yellow and orange clouds around this planet.

Saturn's day and night lasts only 10½ hours, but its year is 29½ Earth years long.

More than twenty moons made of ice orbit Saturn, but its strangest feature is the great flat belt of narrow rings surrounding it in space, rather like grooves in a long-playing record. Most rings are made of specks and chunks of water ice.

Saturn lies nearly ten times farther from the Sun than we do, and nearly twice as far from it as Jupiter. No wonder the cloudy surfaces of these two planets are very cold indeed.

Above The Great Red Spot on Jupiter (top right corner) is believed to be a giant storm system which has survived for at least the past 200 years.

Below The eruption of Io's huge volcano, Pele, (top right corner) throwing a plume of gases 300 km upwards.

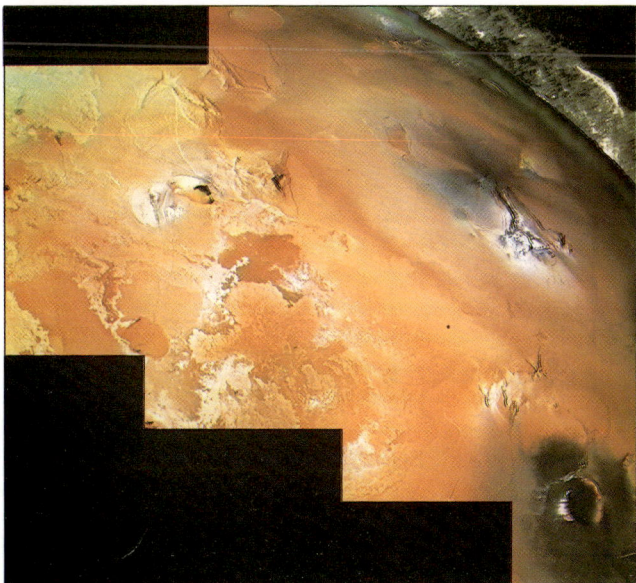

Below The most distinctive feature of Saturn is the belt of rings around it. In this picture three of the planet's icy satellites can be seen: Tethys, Dione and Rhea.

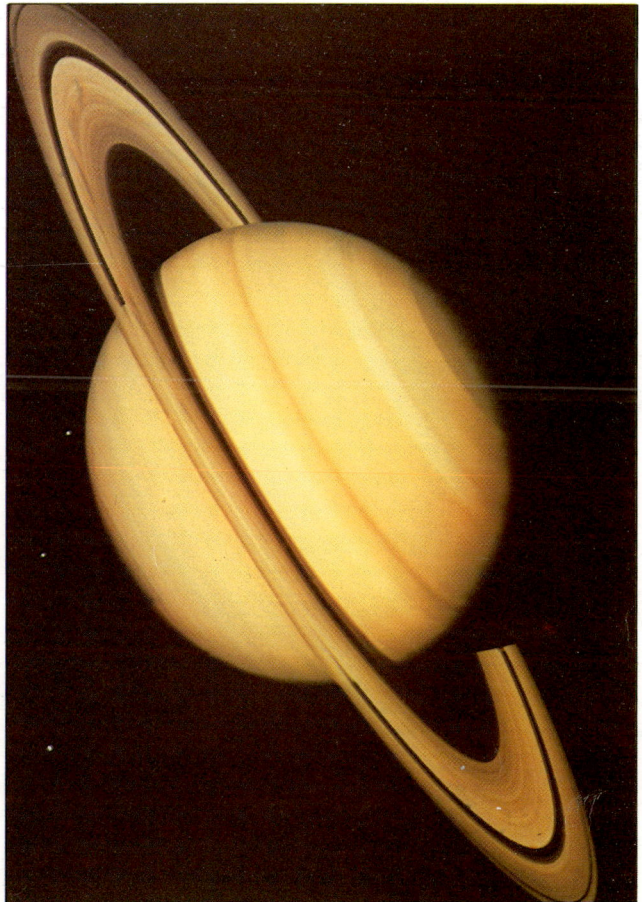

The farthest planets

In 1986 a space probe reached the first of the three most remote planets: Uranus, Neptune and Pluto. Uranus is about nineteen times farther from the Sun than we are. Like Neptune this is a giant bluish-green planet. Only Jupiter and Saturn are larger than Uranus and Neptune. Uranus occupies sixty-seven times more space than the Earth, and Neptune fifty-seven times more. Yet if you could weigh them, Neptune would weigh only seventeen times more than the Earth, and Uranus would be less than fifteen times heavier.

Bulk for bulk, both planets are heavier than Saturn but lighter than the Earth. They might be mostly water covering a rocky core six times as heavy as the Earth. In 1986 pictures sent by *Voyager 2* showed that Uranus has a cold, hazy atmosphere of hydrogen and helium. About twenty rings and fifteen moons are orbiting this planet. Neptune seems to have one broken ring and two moons, maybe more.

Uranus spins lying on its side, so parts have almost everlasting day or night. Uranus and Neptune revolve once every sixteen hours or so. Uranus takes eighty-four Earth years to travel once around the Sun. Neptune's year lasts almost twice that long.

Images of Uranus taken by *Voyager 2*. The left-hand image uses false colour to bring out details in the polar region.

Pluto is the remotest, coldest and smallest planet known. It lies more than thirty times farther from the Sun than we do. From Pluto, the Sun shows as a tiny speck of light. Pluto seems to be a frozen ball of ice and rock smaller than our Moon. Like the Moon this planet has no atmosphere.

A moon called Charon keeps Pluto company. Compared with Pluto's size, Charon is larger than any other planet's moon. Perhaps it broke away from Pluto, or perhaps both once formed a moon of Neptune.

Astronomers think a day and night on Pluto lasts as long as six days and nights on Earth. A year on Pluto equals 247 of our years.

Left An artist's impression of Neptune, seen from Trion, its largest moon.

Below An artist's impression of the moon Charon rising over Pluto. The Sun appears as a distant, bright star.

Specks and rocks

Billions of objects smaller than the moons and planets whizz around the Sun. They range from tiny specks of dust and ice to a 'mini planet' broader than the British Isles.

Specks of space dust are always raining down upon the Earth. Many burn up in the atmosphere as streaks of light called 'shooting stars' or meteors. Pieces large enough to hit the Earth are known as meteorites. About 100 tonnes of tiny meteorites, called micrometeorites, probably arrive unnoticed every day. But only about 150 sizeable meteorites hit the Earth each year. Several thousand of these lumps of rock have been discovered. The largest is a 60-tonne monster found near Hoba West in South West Africa. Huge craters punched into the Earth's crust show where even larger meteorites landed long ago.

There are three main kinds of meteorite, called stones, irons and stony irons. Stones consist of fine-grained stone containing little glassy spheres. Irons are rusty chunks rich in iron and nickel. Stony irons include ingredients found in both the other types. Scientists believe lumps of rock like these were raw materials that helped to build the Earth and Earth-like planets.

Most particles that whizz down to Earth from space are broken bits of asteroids, or so-called minor planets. Astronomers believe that tens of thousands of these asteroids form a belt between Mars and Jupiter. Chiron orbits farther out, between the tracks of Saturn and Uranus. Some people think that Chiron and the 'planet' Pluto are really members of a second, yet to be discovered, belt of asteroids. There are also about 40 so-called apollo asteroids whose strange paths cross the orbit of the Earth.

The largest asteroid is Ceres, a rocky world 1,000 km across. Most others are just stones and boulders tracing out a tumbling path around the Sun. Even if you could put them all together you would build a planet smaller than our Moon.

Above The meteor crater at Winslow, Arizona, USA, which is believed to have been formed about 20,000 years ago when a meteor plunged down to Earth.

TOWER HOUSE SCHOOL

The Geminid meteor (the long, almost vertical bright streak) photographed from California. These night-time showers of 'shooting stars' occur in the same week each year. The short diagonal streaks are star trails.

Comets

Sometimes brilliant objects with a fuzzy head and long bright tail show up in the sky. The ancient Greeks called these 'hairy stars'. From their word for 'hairy' comes our own name 'comets'.

Astronomers believe comets come from the remote edge of the solar system. Out there beyond the planets lies the Oort Cloud – an immense cloud of chunks of ice containing dust and maybe larger particles. Sticking all the chunks together would form a lump no larger than the planet Mars. It is a handful of these 'dirty snowballs' that we see from time to time as comets.

A comet forms like this. First, a passing star's gravitational pull sends a 'dirty snowball' on a path that takes it closer to the Sun. As it nears the Sun, the snowball's ices start evaporating. The evaporating ices glow with reflected sunlight and billow out into a mighty head much bigger than the largest planet, Jupiter. Meanwhile, solar particles and rays drive gas and dust from the comet's nucleus (the snowball). So the comet sprouts a tail of gas and dust that stretches far across the sky. The tail points away from the Sun as the comet travels round it.

The Bayeux Tapestry shows the appearance of Halley's Comet shortly before the Battle of Hastings in 1066.

Above Comet West sprouting a tail of gas (which appears here as blue) and a tail of dust (white) as it shoots across the sky.

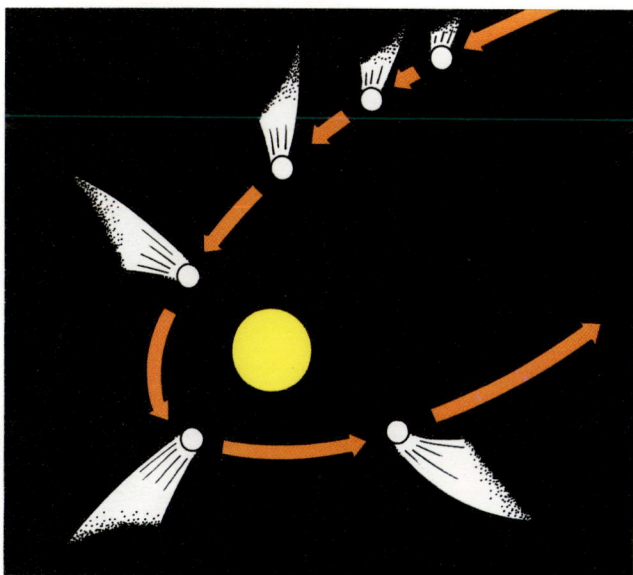

As a comet circles the Sun its tail grows longer. The tail always points away from the Sun.

Sometimes the Earth travels through a comet's tail. So small and scattered are its particles they pass unnoticed. Occasionally, though, a comet's nucleus may strike the Earth head on. Scientists believe a comet zoomed down on Siberia in 1908. Huge explosions flattened a great area of forest, yet the impact left no crater. Most probably the blast came from a comet that melted as it passed down through the atmosphere.

Certain comets follow tracks that bring them into view quite often. For instance Halley's Comet comes around every 76 years. Others trace out longer orbits and appear more rarely. Kohoutek, a comet discovered in 1973, might not show up again for 75,000 years.

The lives of stars

Most of the night sky's innumerable twinkling lights shine from stars. Telescopes reveal millions scattered through space. Many are far larger than our solar system's star, the Sun. They seem so small because they lie so far off. The nearest star is 4.2 light years away. (A light year is the distance light travels in a year – 9.5 million million kilometres.)

Astronomers learn much about the stars from instruments that split starlight into a band of colours called a spectrum. The widths of colours on this band show such things as a star's temperature and whether it moves toward us or away.

Star size and brightness are clues to a star's type and age. All stars form from matter shrinking in a cloud of gas and dust known as a nebula. But stars of different sizes age at different rates and change in different ways. Stars one-tenth as large as ours never really 'take off'. They become dim and red, then fade out. Stars the size of ours are yellow dwarfs that shine steadily for thousands of millions of years. Their energy comes from nuclear reactions turning hydrogen to helium. When a yellow dwarf 'burns' all its hydrogen it swells into a much larger, brighter red giant. When the red giant's energy is gone it collapses into a small dense white dwarf. This may be smaller than our Earth but it is thousands of times heavier.

A new star much bigger than our Sun glows a brilliant blue or white. But it lasts a mere few million years. Then the star explodes as a supernova as bright as 100 million suns. Astronomers believe supernovae leave small, dark, dense fragments called neutron stars. The largest stars of all collapse to leave strange objects called black holes.

Right Seven stages in the life of a star. (1) Nebula cloud of gas and dust. (2) Part of nebula condenses. (3) Yellow dwarf star forms from condensed cloud. (4) Star expands. (5) Star grows into a red giant. (6) Red giant collapses. (7) White dwarf forms from red giant.

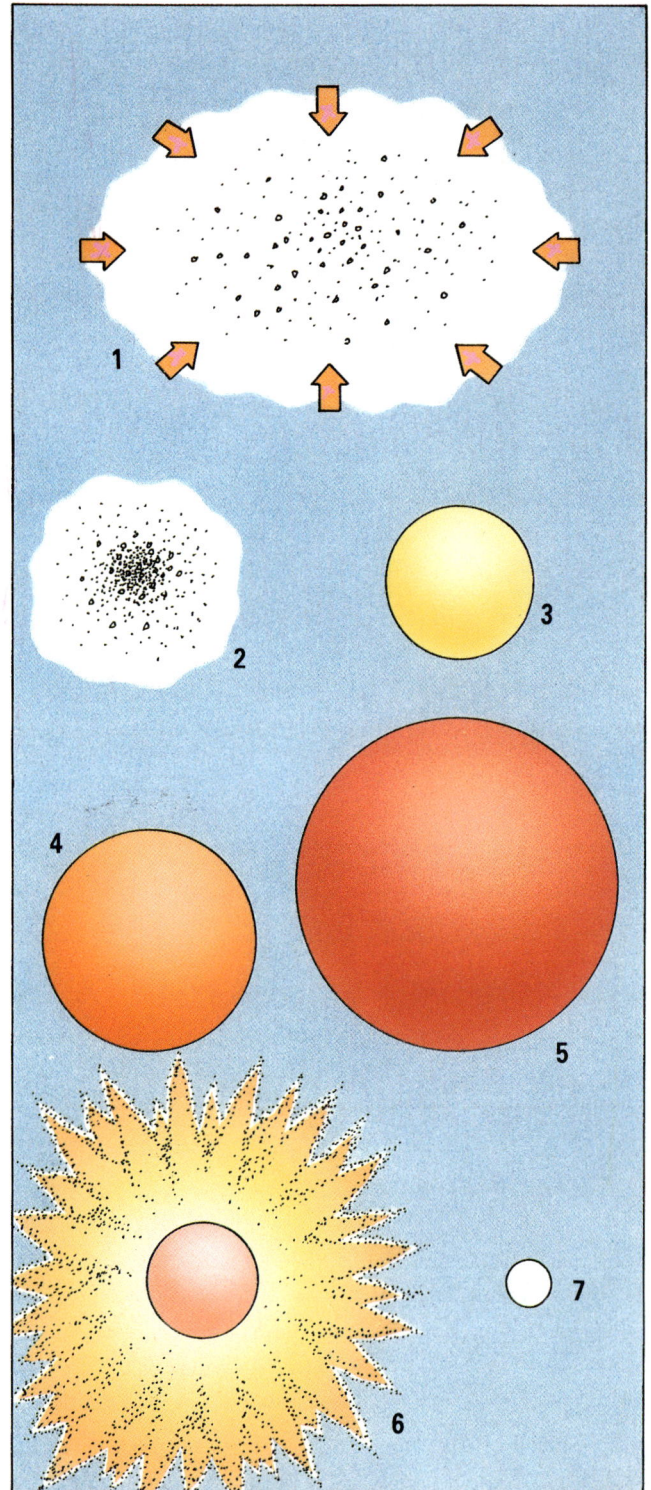

The Orion Nebula, a bright cloud of gas and dust where stars are in the process of being born.

Star groups

Most stars belong to small or large groups. The smallest group is two stars that revolve around one centre of gravity. Astronomers call these pairs binary systems. If one binary star sometimes hides its partner they form an eclipsing binary system. Telescopes have revealed the existence of tens of thousands of binary systems.

Most stars belong to larger groups called multiple systems. Star clusters are groups of stars travelling together through space. An open cluster can hold thousands of stars. A globular cluster is shaped roughly like a globe and can contain up to a million stars.

Binary systems and star clusters can belong to larger groups. Our Sun and about 100,000 million other stars – with nebulae and scattered dust and gas – make up the vast star system called the Galaxy. Most people know it as the Milky Way. On a clear night its mass of stars shows as a pale path across the sky. Black patches in the path are dark

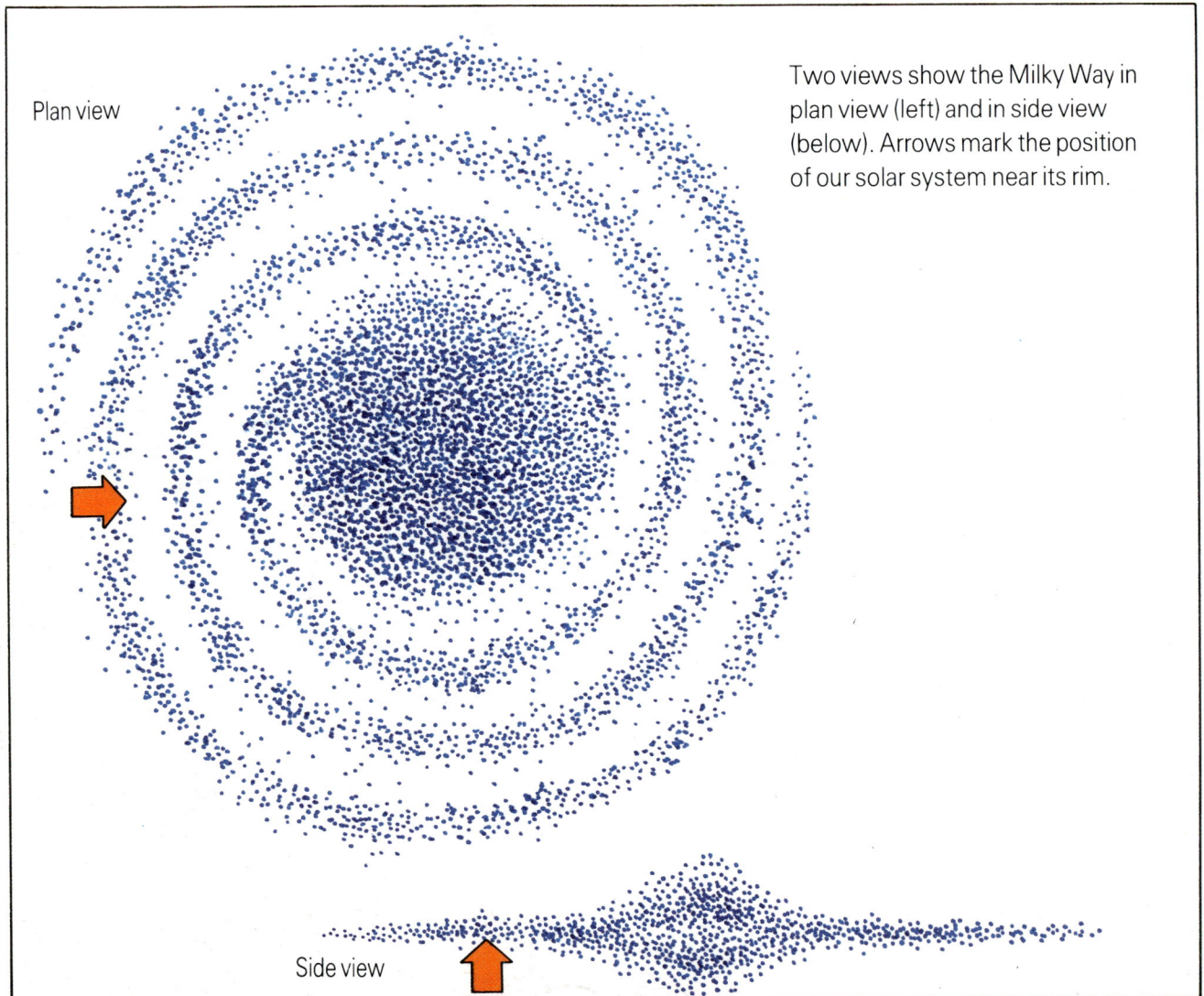

Plan view

Two views show the Milky Way in plan view (left) and in side view (below). Arrows mark the position of our solar system near its rim.

Side view

substances that hide the light of stars beyond. In fact this 'path' is just the Milky Way seen edge-on from the Earth. Seen from another angle it would appear to be a flattish spiral rather like a mighty catherine wheel

The Galaxy might be as much as 100,000 light years across and its bulging middle seems 20,000 light years 'thick'. The Sun lies about 30,000 light years from the centre. This means that light that set off from the middle 30,000 years ago is only reaching us today. Some of the light might well have come from stars that blew up long ago.

The Galaxy is spinning. Our solar system revolves around its centre at more than 790,000 kph. Even so we take 237 million years to complete one turn. We have not yet been once around the centre of the Milky Way since dinosaurs appeared.

A view towards the centre of the Milky Way, showing its many bright star clouds and pink hydrogen nebulae.

Distant galaxies

Far beyond our own great group of stars lie other galaxies. These vast star islands are scattered through the emptiness of space.

Astronomers have noticed that galaxies occur in several shapes. Some are spirals rather like our galaxy, the Milky Way. Among the nearest is the Andromeda Galaxy, a spiral mass of stars 200,000 light years across and 2.2 million light years from the Earth. The Andromeda Galaxy is a normal spiral, with arms projecting from a central bulge.

Barred spirals are galaxies with curved arms that stick out from both ends of a bar-shaped mass of stars. For instance NGC 7479 is a galaxy in the constellation Pegasus. (A constellation is a pattern of stars as seen from Earth.)

Elliptical galaxies range from saucer shaped to spherical. They lack the arms of spiral galaxies.

Irregular galaxies have no clear-cut shape. But some show features seen in other types. For instance the Large Cloud of Magellan, which is an irregular galaxy, has signs of a bar.

Just as groups of stars form galaxies, so galaxies themselves form larger groups. Besides the Milky Way, more than twenty galaxies make up the Local Group, five million light years across.

Some other groups contain far more galaxies. The Virgo cluster, 65 million light years away, holds hundreds or even thousands of galaxies. About 10,000 galaxies make up the Coma cluster more than 100 million light years from the Earth. There are even larger groups of galaxies than that.

Astronomers have detected galaxies 5,000 million light years from the Earth. Galaxies that distant appear as tiny bright smudges. Scientists believe that the universe holds 10,000 million galaxies altogether.

Outside the Local Group all groups of galaxies are separating at a tremendous rate. The farthest objects known are travelling at 8.7 million million kilometres a year – nine-tenths the speed of light. So the whole universe is rapidly expanding.

The Andromeda Galaxy, which together with the Milky Way is one of the largest and most important members of the Local Group of galaxies.

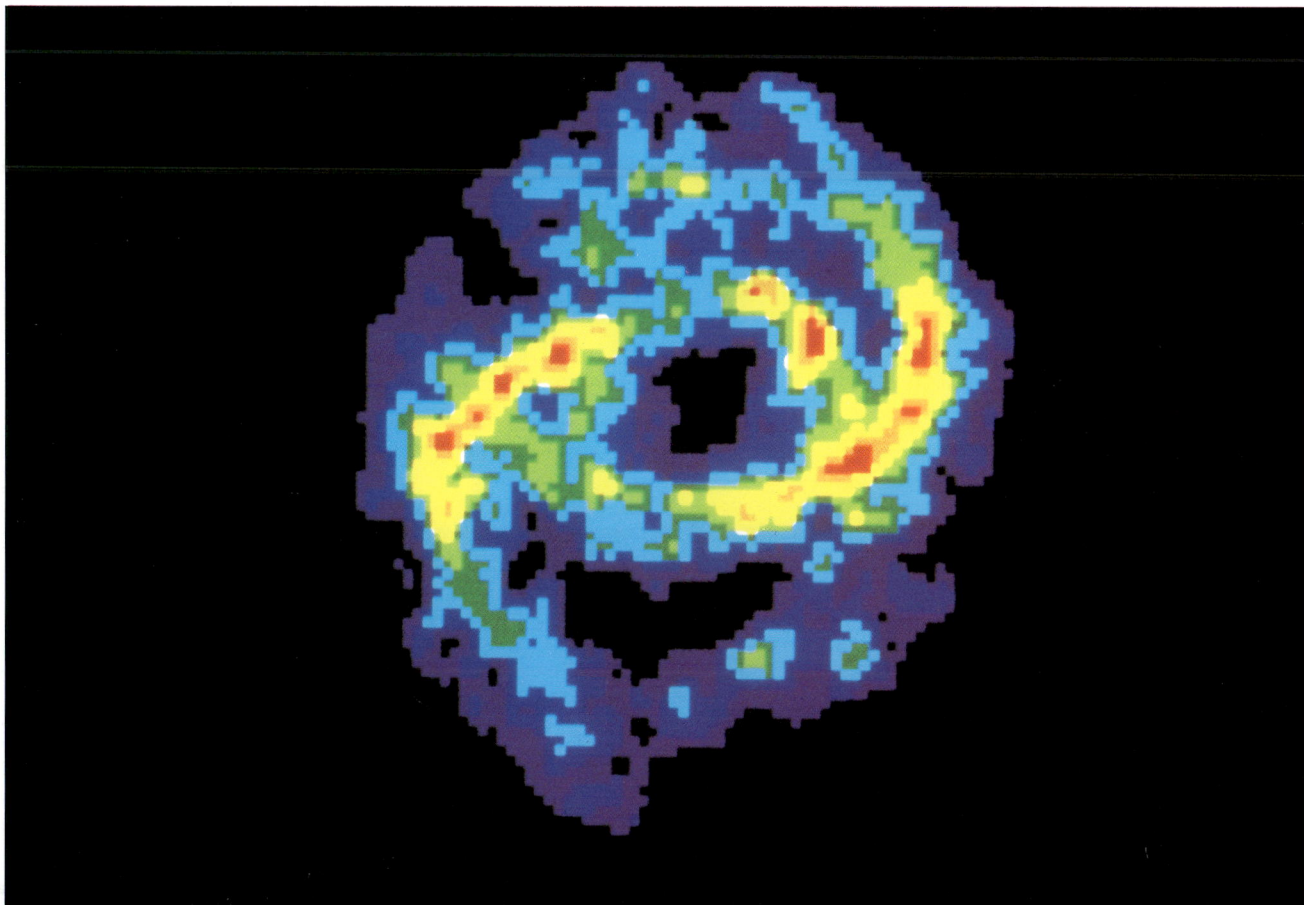

Above A false colour radio map of the barred spiral galaxy NGC 1300. It is colour-coded to show the intensity of emission from the neutral hydrogen within the galaxy.

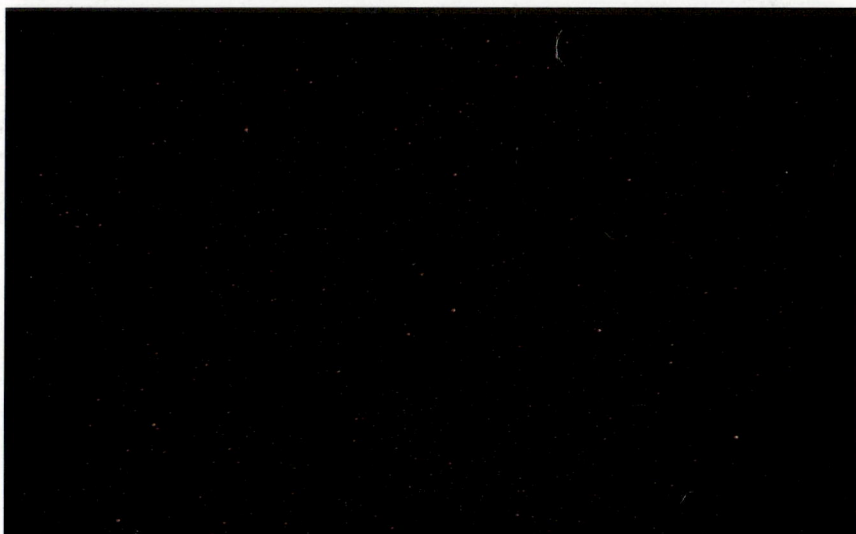

Right The constellation of Pegasus, an extensive constellation in the northern hemisphere, which can be seen from Earth.

Strangers in space

Perhaps the strangest finds in space are pulsars, quasars and black holes.

Pulsar is short for 'pulsating radio source'. Pulsars are small, dense, fast-spinning stars that send out powerful pulses of radio waves. As a pulsar spins, a hot spot on its surface emits radio waves that sweep the sky like a beam of light from a lighthouse. Pulsars release huge quantities of energy, yet many may be only 30 km across. Their main ingredients are closely-packed neutrons, so pulsars are a type of neutron star.

Quasars or quasi-stellar (star-like) radio sources are remote super-bright objects that beam out radio 'noise'. Some are 100 times brighter than the brightest galaxy, although their dazzling cores may be one millionth of its size. Quasars might show us galaxies in the making, long ago. The light arriving from the nearest quasar set out 1,000 million years ago. Other quasars date from close to the beginning of the universe. Quasars include some of the earliest and remotest of all objects.

A computer contrast-enhanced optical image of quasar 3C 273, which is probably the extremely luminous nucleus of a distant galaxy.

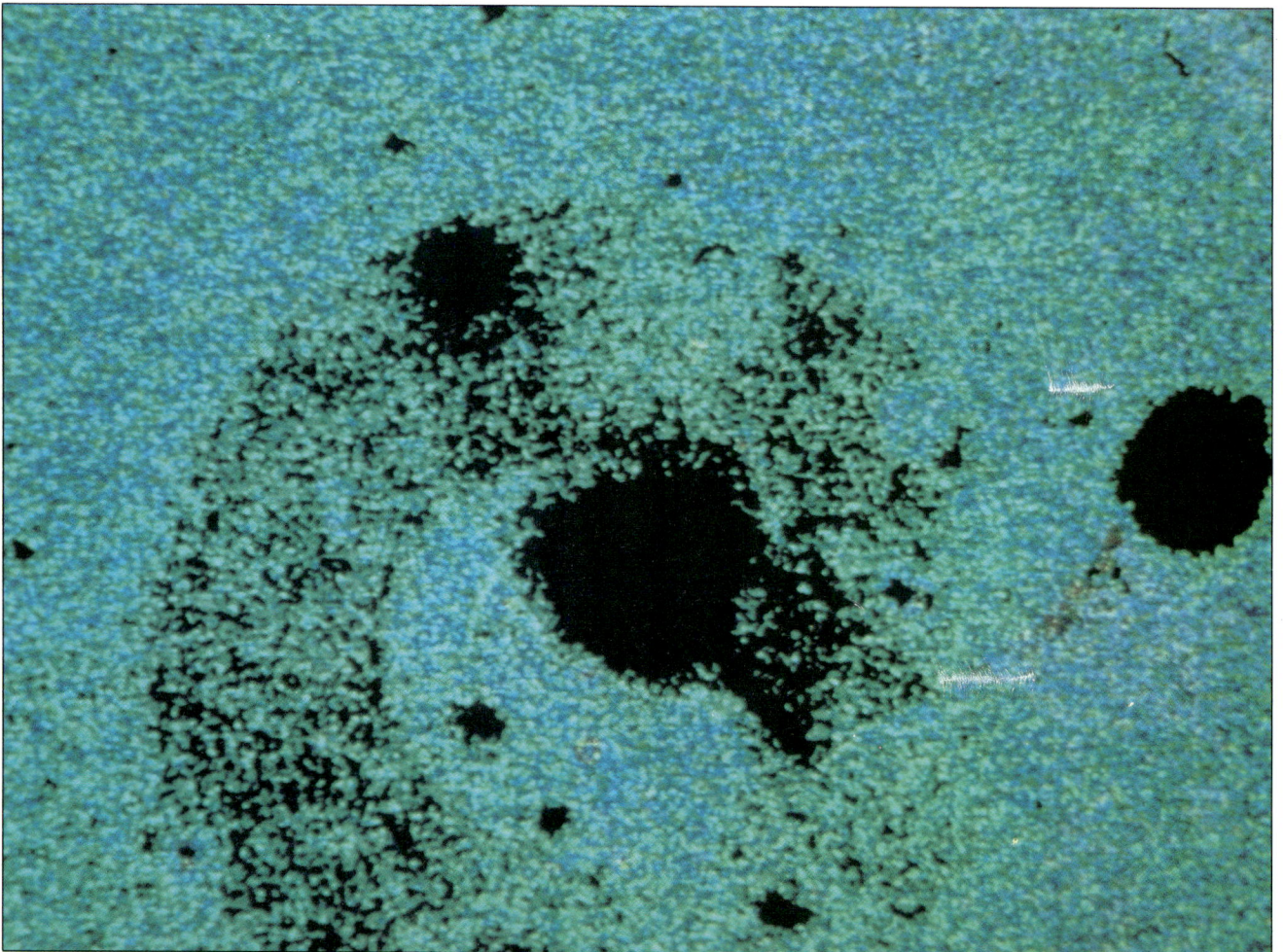

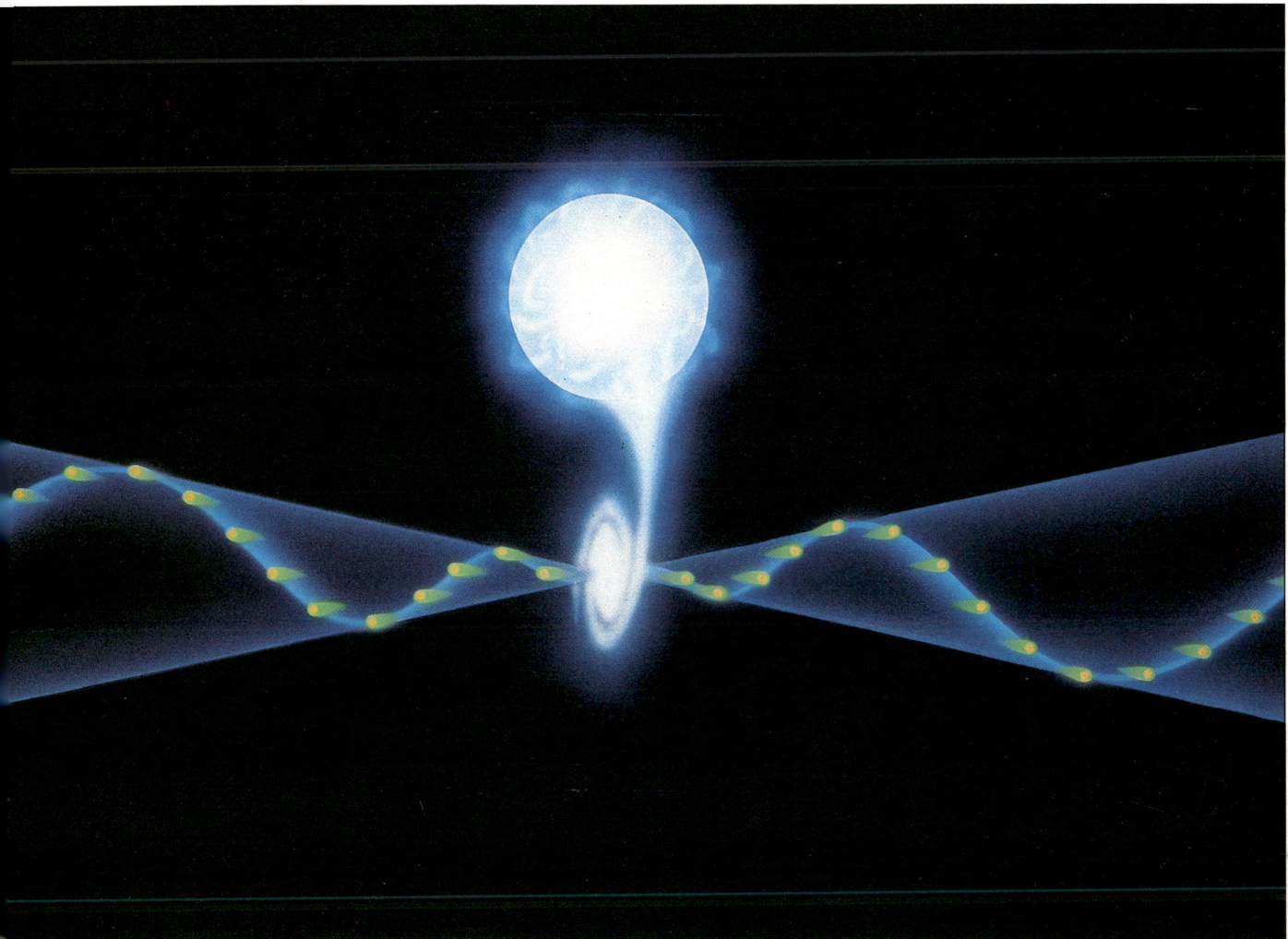

An artist's impression of how a black hole grows and sucks in surrounding stars and gas.

Black holes are thought to be super-dense remains of vast stars that collapsed and shrank. Some are only 6 km across. Others might contain 100 million times as much mass as the Sun. Their intensely powerful gravity stops even light escaping. Black holes are dark mysteries, but scientists can guess how they behave.

Astronomers believe black holes act as whirlpools sucking in surrounding gas and stars.

There may be black holes in the very middle of quasars. Stars that spiral in would break up. This might throw out jets of particles as two immensely long beams projecting from a quasar's core. Such beams make some quasars the largest structures known. One is 25 times larger than our Local Group of galaxies. But its energy could come from a black hole no bigger than our solar system.

Nearer home, astronomers believe a black hole sucks stars into the middle of the Milky Way. Many million years from now a black hole might gobble up the Sun and planets.

The Crab Nebula, an expanding supernova remnant, is a nebula that radiates radio waves and light for hundreds of thousands of years.

Glossary

Asteroid A stony or metallic object orbiting the Sun. Asteroids are sometimes known as minor planets.

Atmosphere The gases surrounding a star, planet or moon.

Atom The smallest particle of matter that can take part in a chemical reaction.

Axis An imaginary line about which a planet, moon or other body rotates.

Big Bang The immense explosion thought to have produced the universe.

Binary stars Two stars revolving around the same centre of gravity.

Biosphere The part of the Earth inhabited by living things.

Black hole The dark, dense remains of an immense star that has collapsed. A black hole's force of gravity is so great that not even light escapes.

Chromosphere The Sun's lower atmosphere just above its photosphere.

Comet A lump of dust and frozen gases that sprouts a glowing tail as it circles the Sun.

Constellation A group of stars in an imaginary outline supposed to resemble a god, animal or other object.

Core In astronomy, the middle of a star, planet or moon.

Crust The solid surface of an Earth-like planet or a moon.

Density The mass of a given volume of some substance, measured as grams per cubic centimetre.

Eclipse This occurs when a sun, planet or moon passes in front of another heavenly body, hiding it from view.

Element A substance made of atoms of the same kind.

Equator An imaginary east-west line around the middle of a planet, sun or moon.

Galaxies Great systems of stars.

Galaxy The great star system that includes the solar system. It is also called the Milky Way.

Gravity The force with which one object attracts another. It is also called gravitation.

Hemisphere Half the Earth or half another heavenly body.

Light year The distance that light travels in one year.

Local Group The group of galaxies that includes our own galaxy, the Galaxy or Milky Way.

Magnetic field The area of magnetic force around the Earth or another object behaving as a magnet.

Mantle A hot rock layer between the core and crust of a planet or a moon.

Mass The amount of matter making up an object. Mass differs from weight. An astronaut's weight varies with the pull of gravity on Earth, in space and on the Moon. But the astronaut's mass remains the same everywhere.

Meteor A particle from space that burns up as it falls down through the Earth's atmosphere.

Meteorite A metallic or stony lump that lands on Earth from space. Meteorites also fall on other planets and their moons.

Moon A heavenly body orbiting a planet. Moons are also known as satellites.

Nebula A cloud of gas and dust from which stars form.

Neutron star A small, dense star mainly made of neutrons.

Nuclear reaction A change that involves an atom's nucleus. Nuclear fusion reactions give stars their energy and make new elements.

Nucleus The vital central point of an object.

Orbit The curved path of one heavenly body around another.

Photosphere The Sun's fiery surface.

Planet A large, dark heavenly body orbiting a star.

Planetesimals Rocky and metallic lumps like asteroids, once orbiting the Sun. Planetesimals probably came together to produce the Earth and Earth-like planets.

Poles Imaginary points on the Earth's surface at each end of the Earth's axis.

Pulsar A neutron star emitting rapidly varying radio waves.

Quasar A remote, bright type of object, perhaps a galaxy in the making.

Red giant An ageing ordinary star that glows red as its core shrinks and its surface expands.

Satellite A planet or body in space that orbits around a larger one. The Earth is a satellite of the Sun.

Solar corona The outer atmosphere of the Sun.

Solar flares Radiation erupting in the Sun's chromosphere.

Solar prominences Glowing gases erupting through the solar corona.

Solar system The sun and the planets, moons and other objects orbiting around it.

Solar wind Electrically charged particles speeding from the Sun through the solar system.

Space probe A device sent from the Earth to explore other objects in the solar system.

Spectrum The coloured bands produced when white light is split up by a prism or similar device.

Star A sun. Most stars are intensely hot and bright.

Star cluster A group of stars moving together through space. A star cluster is smaller than a galaxy.

Subatomic particles Particles smaller than or forming parts of atoms.

Sun A star.

Sunspots Relatively cool, dark markings on the Sun's photosphere.

Supernova A brilliant, massive star in the process of exploding.

Tropics Parallel east-west circles around the Earth about 23½ degrees from the equator – about one quarter of the way to the Poles.

Universe All matter, space and energy.

White dwarf A tiny, dense star that has collapsed after its nuclear reactions stopped.

Yellow dwarf An ordinary star like the Sun, in a long, steady stage of its life.

Further reading

Couper, Heather, with Henbest, Nigel *The Planets* (Pan Books 1985)

Francis, Peter *The Planets* (Penguin Books 1981)

Kerrod, Robin *The Universe* (Sampson Low 1975)

Lambert, David *The Solar System* (Wayland 1984)

Mitchell, James (general editor) *The Joy of Knowledge Encyclopaedia* (Mitchell Beazley 1980)

Patrick Moore's Pocket Guide to the Stars and Planets (Mitchell Beazley 1982)

Picture acknowledgements

The publishers would like to thank the following for allowing their photographs to be reproduced in this book: Bruce Coleman Limited 12 below (Hans Reinhard), 14 above (Leonard Lee Rue III), 14 below (Jen and Des Bartlett), 15 above (L.C. Marigo), 15 below (Gene Ahrens), 24, 31 below (Michael Freeman); Michael Holford 34; Ann Ronan Picture Library 5 (both); Science Photo Library 11 (Martin Dohrn), 12 above (Sinclair Stammers), 19 above (High Altitude Observatory of National Centre for Atmospheric Research, Boulder, Colorado), 22 (NASA), 23 (both) (NASA), 25 (NASA), 26 (NASA), 27 (both) (NASA), 28 (NASA), 29 (all three) (NASA), 30 (NASA), 31 above (David A. Hardy), 32–3 (John Sanford), 33 (Jerry Mason), 35 (Ronald Royer), 37 (Ronald Royer), 39 (Fred Espenak), 40 (NASA), 41 above (Dr Martin W. England), 41 below (John Sanford), 42 (Malina Kea Observatory, University of Hawaii/S. Wyckoff & P.A. Wehinger), 43 (David Parker), 44 (US Naval Observatory), front cover (inset), back cover; Ronald Sheridan Ancient Art and Architecture Collection 4; ZEFA 19 below (Photri), 21 (Photri), front cover (main picture). All illustrations are by Stefan Chabluk.

Index